April 13, 1997

To Nate

Happy Birthday. [...]
you often. Enjoy the game
of baseball. It was my game
in my youth.

Love Grandpa

MURPH

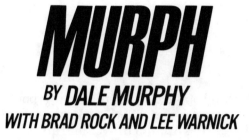

MURPH

BY DALE MURPHY
WITH BRAD ROCK AND LEE WARNICK

Bookcraft
Salt Lake City, Utah

Many of the photographs in this book
are reprinted herein courtesy of
the Atlanta Braves and are
used with permission.

Library of Congress Catalog Card Number: 86-70916
ISBN 0-88494-598-7

4th Printing, 1989

Printed in the United States of America

CONTENTS

Part III Perspectives

INTRODUCTION

The sun, weak and beaten, was setting on January 20, 1985, in Atlanta. A chill wind swept across central Georgia, temperatures holding near zero. The worst cold snap in a century had gripped a city unaccustomed to the irritations of black ice and frostbite. Cars stalled along the freeway; tow trucks took in a big business. Restaurants were sparsely populated, and some patrons wore coats even indoors.

We took I–285 north towards Roswell, but after five miles and no sign of heat from our rental car we drove back and exchanged it.

The rent-a-car business wasn't ready for the cold, either.

Arriving in Roswell we turned down a quarter-mile paved lane, the car lights cutting through a stand of protective white oaks and pines and glancing off a small pond. We pulled up to Dale and Nancy Murphy's stately home on a circular driveway.

Before the engine was shut off, Dale was out of the door.

"I was really starting to worry," he began. "The bad weather . . . I didn't know if you would be able to find your way all right in the dark."

Introductions followed. "Here," he said, "let me help you with the luggage."

This was our first meeting with the baseball player many consider to be the best in the game today. We found him to be unaffected, unpretentious, and sincere.

The Murphys had insisted we stay at their home instead of a hotel to avoid numerous trips back and forth for interviews. By the time we arrived, their children—Chad, Travis, and Shawn—had gone to bed, so we talked for an hour before retiring.

Dale asked what time we wanted to start interviews the next morning, saying he would be back around 8:00 A.M.

"Back from where?"

He explained casually that he taught an early-morning seminary class for the LDS church every weekday during the off-season. For this assignment he rises at 5:15; no small task, especially considering the late hours major league ballplayers must keep. Late nights on the job means sleeping late the next day—a hard habit to break in the off-season.

Dale takes it without a hint of complaint or concern.

Since meeting Dale we have realized, as have many others, just how deep his religious convictions are—and how seriously he lives by them. His treatment of family and stranger alike remains constant, his dedication to do what's right unwavering.

Hence there is no controversy, no sensational "telling-all" in Dale Murphy's autobiography; nor should there be. Such an account would be a gross distortion. Dale's style is not negative or self-important. If other superstars take a different tack, it reflects their philosophies of life, as Dale's story reflects his.

Dale's concerns are not the faults of owners or the quirks of other players. His attitudes, though less colorful than those of other highly publicized players, are still quite unusual in the fast-lane frenzy of professional sports. His ability to live by his principles while consistently performing with the best players in baseball makes him an intriguing personality. He is a rare commodity in the dollar- and ego-inflated professional world, a truly gifted athlete who realizes his talents *are* a gift.

At a time when almost everyone of note seems to have an exposé to publish, some inside gossip about himself or others to share with a hungry public, Dale, too, has something to share. If less sensational, it is far more wholesome.

His beliefs are not something he professes merely to build up his public image; in fact at one stage in his career Dale was willing to give up his entire future in baseball to honor those beliefs. They would remain the same whether he was a millionaire baseball hero or a convenience-store clerk.

Dale's concerns are for his family, his church, and his fellow man, as well as for the game he adores. In a way not so common these days, yet still valid, Dale Murphy is a true individual. A genuine article.

Athletes in bigger media centers may receive greater coverage, but Dale is arguably the most popular athlete in America with the press. Rarely is a writer or sportscaster unimpressed with the sincerity and regard with which he treats them. This has usually resulted in extremely favorable reporting.

Twenty-five years ago such gushing over an athlete was not uncommon. Writers portrayed athletes as legendary folk heroes, glorifying their on-field accomplishments and turning their backs on off-field quirks—or even outrages.

Those days are gone, yet no one has found reason to believe that Dale is not what he appears to be. It is indeed a rarity to see an athlete under so much scrutiny receiving so much laudatory coverage. Cynical journalists are refreshed by this family man who owns up to the realization that how he plays baseball isn't the most important thing on the planet.

Despite the countless awards and honors bestowed on him, he remains unimpressed with himself. Just inside the front door of his home is a den where we conducted interviews with Dale. Behind the desk is a large gun cabinet, set into the wall by the builder of the home. Since Dale doesn't keep guns, friends have suggested he make it into a trophy case.

"I've been after him to make something to keep his awards in, but I don't know if he'll ever do it," says his close friend and former next-door neighbor Chris Callaway.

Several bats are stashed in the gun rack, but none are mementos of his hitting accomplishments. They are bats he has collected at All-Star games, autographed by either former or current major league stars.

While hanging his clothes in the walk-in closet adjoining his room the first night, Lee Warnick noticed something shining in a box on the floor. Stooping to look more closely, he saw it was a gold-painted baseball glove, one of the four coveted Gold Glove awards Dale has earned in his career. Rather than displaying his honors in a prominent place, he feels more comfortable stashing them in a closet on the third floor of his home.

Dale's popularity isn't limited to the media. He is a favorite among teammates—who tease him about his size-thirteen feet and his appetite—and among neighbors and civic and religious leaders. Not only has he been recognized as a faithful member of the LDS church, but he has been written up in *Guideposts*, an inter-denominational religious publication, as exemplifying a Christian life-style.

All of this Dale downplays.

"No matter what people might think about religion in sports," said former teammate Bob Watson in one newspaper article, "he has a strong conviction and I'd like to see more people like that. Dale Murphy is a man's man, and I think the

youngsters out there who read and see things about Dale don't
see anything bad about him. He's a guy they can definitely look
to as an example."

Even after a number of years enjoying the affluence of major
league baseball, Dale remains untainted by wealth. He normally
wears jeans, tennis shoes, and a golf shirt; and though he earns
well over a million dollars a year, he is quick to admit baseball
salaries are way out of perspective. Big salaries, he says, should
go to teachers, police officers, and the like. "Dale thinks what
players make today can get out of line," says his father, Charles
Murphy.

There are few visible signs of the Murphys' wealth. The
family recently moved from a subdivision in Lawrenceville to a
more secluded home in Roswell. It is a large, but not palatial,
three-story English country house amid ten acres of woods.
"Dale and Nancy use their money mainly to buy privacy," says
Dale's sister, Susan.

Several years ago Dale made a small concession to his tremendous earning power by buying himself a Corvette, the
dream of every American boy in the past three decades.

"He wouldn't drive it, though," says his friend Chris. "It was
months before he'd even take it to church. Finally I pulled him
aside and said, 'Dale, people know who you are. You aren't
flashy. You aren't a show-off. There is no need to apologize
because you own a Corvette.' A couple of weeks later he finally
drove it to church."

Often Dale's parents in Portland are asked if he showers
them with expensive gifts, but his gift-buying tastes haven't
changed much since high school. One year he bought his father
a four-dollar digital watch in Philadelphia for a birthday
present. "Dale just loved it. Thought it was the neatest thing in
the world," laughs his father. "How much a gift costs is not the
important thing to Dale."

One Christmas he sent his sister and her husband a fifty-
gallon drum to store water in, though neither are Mormons. "At
first we didn't know what to think," she said, "but then we
realized what those things meant to him and we were touched."

Dale is so unconcerned about money, he rarely carries much
with him. "He'll go down to the corner store to get some milk
and won't have a nickel on him," says Chris. "He'll either ask
me to lend it to him if I'm with him or they'll just say, 'Go ahead,

Dale, we know you're good for your money. Bring it in next time.' "

There are no false airs of self-importance about him, something even those who know Dale only casually will attest to. "He didn't change a bit when he became a baseball star. Not a bit. We had to pry things out of him," says Dale's high school baseball coach, Jack Dunn. "And I can still bawl him out for doing something wrong. As his old coach I've told him I retain all yelling rights. It's great to be able to yell at the [former] MVP of the National League."

When the Murphys were still living next to the Callaways in Lawrenceville, Dale called his neighbor in the middle of the night to borrow a thermometer because one of the kids was sick.

"Sure," said Chris, "I'll bring it right over."

"No, no, let me come get it."

"No, Dale, I can run it over."

"No, I won't let you do that. Tell you what. I'll meet you halfway."

When they left their garages and turned on the yard lights between the homes, "It looked like two heads of state at a summit meeting," recalls Chris. "Dale came walking out wearing his robe. When he got up close I couldn't stop laughing. It was a Sunday night and he hadn't been able to find the belt for his robe, so he had pulled his necktie — the one he had worn to church that day — around his waist. We just stood there and laughed."

Dale doesn't stand on ceremony. He is, however, a man of principle who stands up for what he believes. It has been well recorded how a fan was shouting from the box seats during one game when Dale approached the screen and said, "You can say what you want, but don't cuss."

"And that," former Braves manager Joe Torre was quoted as saying, "was the last we heard from that particular gentleman."

Through his beliefs Dale has earned the respect of his teammates. Year-end team parties, normally held on Sundays, have been rescheduled so Dale could attend.

Dr. Claude Thomas, Nancy's father, tells of sitting at a game near the Braves' owner, Ted Turner. "He turned around to us and said, 'You know, I'm not a bad guy. I believe in God and I try to treat people honestly. I give to charities. I'm a pretty good guy. But I'm not like Dale. Dale's a saint. Is there anybody in the world like Dale? All you Mormons aren't like Dale, I know.' "

Dale generously donates both time and money to the LDS Church and to many charities. For example, Linda Wride, a family friend, required a heart transplant and in the process her family accumulated staggering medical bills. Dale chaired a drive to help pay off those bills and in a few months quietly cleared the debt, in part with his own money.

"Dale is like you're supposed to be in the storybooks, and you can't quite believe it," says Dr. Thomas. "It's even hard for us to believe it, right now, even after all these years."

In a 1984 *Sport Magazine* article a prominent advertising executive sighed that Murphy's image is of "a guy from 1954," and that he is just not marketable in these times. Many would disagree. But marketability is not a concern for Dale Murphy.

"The one Brave who is himself with no airs, and who isn't stricken by a degree of self-importance, is Murphy," wrote *Atlanta Journal* columnist Furman Bisher. "Let me simply say that I have never met an athlete I admire more. That is pure respect for a young man by an old man who recommends that what this country needs is a big change if Dale's kind of heroism isn't important in these times."

After all the plaudits have been handed down and the years have passed, Dale's concern — then as now — will be his performance as a husband, as a father, and as a Latter-day Saint. When all the lights are turned down and the ink has long since dried, he will be no different than he is now, in the summer of his career.

So we learn what we can from this compelling man who has given to the world much more than just a growing list of impressive baseball statistics and awards. He has given an example. Everyone who knows Dale comes to the same, inevitable conclusion drawn by a friend, who says, shaking his head: "Gentlemen, I'm afraid the problem is that there is just not enough Murph to go around."

BRAD ROCK
LEE WARNICK

Professional Career Statistics

Batting statistics

Year	Team	G	AB	R	H	2B	3B	HR	RBI	BB	SO	SB	BA	SA
1974	Kingsport	54	181	28	46	7	0	5	31	24	53	0	.254	.376
1975	Greenwood	131	443	48	101	20	1	5	48	36	63	5	.228	.312
1976	Savannah	104	352	37	94	13	5	12	55	25	61	6	.267	.435
1976	Richmond	18	50	10	13	1	1	4	8	1	12	0	.260	.560
1977	Richmond	127	466	71	142	33	4	22	90	33	64	4	.305	.534
Minor league		434	1492	194	396	74	11	48	232	119	253	15	.265	.426
1976	Atlanta	19	65	3	17	6	0	0	9	7	9	0	.262	.354
1977	Atlanta	18	76	5	24	8	1	2	14	0	8	0	.316	.526
1978	Atlanta	151	530	66	120	14	3	23	79	42	145	11	.226	.394
1979	Atlanta	104	384	53	106	7	2	21	57	38	67	6	.276	.469
1980	Atlanta	156	569	98	160	27	2	33	89	59	133	9	.281	.510
1981	Atlanta	104	369	43	91	12	1	13	50	44	72	14	.247	.390
1982	Atlanta	162	598	113	168	23	2	36	109	93	134	23	.281	.507
1983	Atlanta	162	589	131	178	24	4	36	121	90	110	30	.302	.540
1984	Atlanta	162	607	94	176	32	8	36	100	79	134	19	.290	.547
1985	Atlanta	162	616	118	185	32	2	37	111	90	141	10	.300	.539
Major league		1200	4403	724	1225	185	25	237	739	542	953	122	.278	.493

League championship series

Year	Location	G	AB	R	H	2B	3B	HR	RBI	BB	SO	SB	BA
1982	vs. St. Louis	3	11	1	3	0	0	0	0	0	2	1	.273

All-star game

1980	at L.A.	1	1	0	0	0	0	0	0	.000
1982	at Montreal	1	2	1	0	0	0	1	0	.000
1983	at Chicago	1	3	0	0	1	1	0	1	.333
1984	at S.F.	1	3	1	0	0	1	1	0	.667
1985	at Minnesota	1	3	0	0	0	0	0	1	.333
All-star game totals		5	12	2	0	1	2	2	2	.333

Fielding statistics

Year	Pos.	G	PO	A	E	TC	DP	Pct.
1976	C	18	114	11	6	131	2	.954
1977	C	19	100	13	3	116	0	.974
1978	1B	129	1137	92	20	1249	84	.984
	C	21	83	13	3	99	0	.970
1979	1B	76	685	42	15	742	61	.980
	C	27	127	15	5	147	2	.966
1980	OF	154	374	14	6	394	4	.985
	1B	1	10	1	0	11	0	1.000
1981	OF	103	254	11	5	270	4	.981
	1B	3	10	0	0	10	1	1.000
1982	OF	162	407	6	9	422	2	.979
1983	OF	160	373	10	6	389	0	.985
1984	OF	160	369	10	5	379	1	.987
1985	OF	161	334	8	7	349	4	.980
Totals:	C	85	424	52	17	493	4	.966
	1B	209	1842	135	35	2012	146	.983
	OF	900	2111	59	38	2203	15	.985

Part I

Early Years

1 Taking the Safe Road

Hayhurst Elementary School, Portland, Oregon. I was having a blast playing Peewee League baseball. It was my first year of organized baseball, and I was playing in pretty much every game. Of course, so was everybody else.

I had one big problem, though.

I couldn't hit.

I just could not hit, and for some reason—I don't know exactly why—I struck out a lot. In fact, I got only one hit the entire year: a double. Getting a double was no major accomplishment when you consider that anytime you get wood on the ball in Peewee League, you have a good chance of going for two bases, even on an infield grounder.

I couldn't hit the ball, but strangely enough I didn't care. I was never too upset about it. As I got older I started realizing I was supposed to catch *and* hit the ball, but at the time I didn't really grasp what was going on.

It was the same with my grades in school. I didn't really get good grades, but I'm not sure I had the idea that I was supposed to. I would just go to school and enjoy myself. In baseball I would just go out and play. It was fun just being there.

There was one time I got extremely upset. I was pitching and accidentally hit my best friend, Jeff Dunn, in the back. He was up there at the plate, batting left-handed, and I threw it into the middle of his back. He dropped the bat and started crying; so did I. All the strikeouts of the season didn't come close to bothering me as much as hitting Jeff with a pitch.

At that stage one thing was apparent. I was no child baseball prodigy. I was small and wiry. My dad used to say I looked like a starving kid from India—skinny with a potbelly.

When I was four, Dad tried to teach me how to throw a baseball but finally gave up. Playing the game didn't interest me nearly as much as watching it. I would sit in front of the television even at that age and watch whole games. One day, while watching a Boston Red Sox game, I saw an outfielder catch the ball and throw it back to the infield. I picked up a ball and said to Dad, "Like this?"

I finally threw a ball.

We lived in a little three-bedroom ranch-style home with brick and shake siding on Idaho Street in Portland. It was a quiet, hilly neighborhood and the back yard was maybe two hundred feet deep. Except for the fruit trees, it was an ideal place to hit fly balls.

I had only one sibling, my sister, Susan, who was three years older. In the early years when I was still learning baseball, Dad would hit flies to us out back. Susan was interested in softball, and most of the backyard practice was to help her develop her softball skills, not to make me into any rising star. They just kind of let me in on it.

There were also a lot of neighborhood games in the street, but they didn't work out so well. Somebody would hit the ball too far and it would roll all the way down the hill. Though I had a lot of neighborhood friends, I never got very close to them. I would go to school and play with those friends, then go home and play with the kids on Idaho Street.

Since we were the only two children in the family, Susan and I were close. We never fought much because I mostly went along with what she wanted.

As we grew older we stayed close, despite being quite different. She was an excellent student, strong-willed and determined. I was sports-oriented, easy-going, and more lax in my studies. Though Susan was a good student, she always liked sports, too. Dad took her to see The King and His Court softball team, then bought her a softball and taped a strike zone on the basement wall for her to practice throwing against.

By the time we got to high school—I was a freshman when she was a senior—she had grown kind of protective about me and I was something of a pest. We didn't talk about deep things too much, because she rarely saw me without one of my baseball friends—usually Jeff. I didn't often talk to her about girlfriends or life. We just got along.

Of course, I wanted to get along with everybody. I didn't like controversy. During my second grade year Mom attended a parent-teacher conference and noted that my desk was off by itself in the schoolroom. She asked the teacher if everything was all right or if I had been getting into trouble. The teacher said I wasn't in any trouble, but she had to put me off there by myself because she couldn't keep the other kids from talking to me.

For some reason, school was a rather confusing matter to me. I didn't get *F*'s or anything that drastic, but I don't think I ever really understood what I was supposed to be doing. My grades weren't as good as they could have been, and I got into a habit of talking too much. I wasn't always paying attention.

That lasted through high school.

Jeff Dunn was always my best friend. We met in kindergarten, and he was the first kid who ever invited me to sleep over at his house. We started out playing at recess and after school, ended up on the same baseball and basketball teams, and in our spare time played "whiffleball" with the other guys. We had some pretty intense "whiffleball" games. We'd get twenty or twenty-five feet away from each other and fire the ball as hard as we could. The ball had holes in it that made it dip and curve all over the place. It was good practice, and before long we could hit it regularly.

That tradition of playing "whiffleball" started in grade school and lasted past high school . . . way past high school. My old friends still play it. I haven't been able to get into one of their games since I turned professional, and I'm a little afraid to. They're so good, they'd probably embarrass me.

Neither Jeff nor I were serious troublemakers. Alpenrose Dairy was near our house; sometimes we'd go over there and sneak around where we weren't supposed to be, but generally I was . . . well, chicken. Whenever it came to the argument,

"Well, the worst they can do is kick us out," I would back down.
I didn't like confrontations and wouldn't go. Taking chances
wasn't my idea of a good time.

When I was very little I did start a small fire in our back yard
on Idaho Street, and somehow I got the idea that just a little bit
of gas might help. When I threw it on, the fire poofed up and
singed my hair. I was terrified. Susan and I put the fire out—
luckily it wasn't a huge fire—but, man, I was scared to death. I
was washing my face when Mom came in and saw that a clump
of my hair was all curled and burnt.

"What's been going on?"

I told her right then and there, like a good boy.

Besides, she had all the evidence she needed.

Jeff and I were usually in it together when mischief was
made. Once in high school we were playing ball on the lawn
next to the school instead of on the baseball field, and I hit a
rising line drive through the principal's office window. Nothing
much came of it though. Then there were the times when Jeff
would put on a gorilla mask, wrap a fur coat around himself,
and climb on my shoulders. We'd go to basketball games or
walk past the school library windows and get big laughs. That
was about the time "Bigfoot" was a popular topic in the North-
west.

We did nothing that would get us in trouble with the law. We
even stayed away from high school fights. Whenever we'd play
a basketball game somewhere and hear that there was going to
be a big rumble afterwards, we would avoid it. There was plenty
of that going on if we had wanted to be part of it. In fact, they
switched some of our football and basketball games from night
to afternoon to avoid trouble. There were also drugs available at
Wilson High, but we didn't mess with them.

Confrontations made me uneasy. I vaguely remember once
punching a guy—well, I didn't really hit him in the face, but just
kind of elbowed him good—but I've never really been in a fight.
It may seem strange for an athlete, but I've never been in a
knockdown, drag-out fistfight. I avoid fights at all costs.

Somewhere I learned the lesson that it doesn't pay to fight. I
even got a lesson when I didn't earn it. In my first year of pro
baseball at Kingsport, Tennessee, the team had a rule: If you
went on the field during a brawl it was a fifty-dollar fine. If you
picked up a bat, it was another fifty dollars. One night during a
game a fight started. I saw a bat on the ground near the fighters

and thought someone might get out of hand and try to use it as a weapon. I came out of the dugout to get the bat.

That cost me fifty dollars.

Then I picked up the bat and returned it to the dugout.

That cost me another fifty dollars.

I guess there was a principle involved.

2 M-U-R-P-H

My parents, Charles and Betty Murphy, instilled in me my sense of right and wrong. They never forced me to play sports or made me feel that I had to win. They just told me to have fun and do what's right. I think the reason why I never got in much trouble was the loyalty I felt to them.

We never had any big talks about right and wrong, but by watching them I could tell what I should and should not do.

Both had solid, hardworking Midwestern values; both were products of lower middle–class homes. Mom grew up in Okemah, Oklahoma, the daughter of schoolteachers. She was born in 1929 and lived through the Depression. There was always food for their family, but never any extra.

My dad was born in 1928 in Cozad, Nebraska, the son of a construction worker. When he was thirteen, Dad's family moved to Richland, Washington, where his father worked with the plutonium projects. Mom's family arrived a couple of years later. Shortly after, they met. They attended Washington State University and were married during Dad's senior year of college, while he pursued a degree in electrical engineering.

Everybody always called my dad "Murph." When I was small I used to look at his lunch bucket with *M-U-R-P-H* painted across the side and wish I had my own — the lettering on the side included. Mom still calls Dad "Murph."

In 1951 Westinghouse hired Dad and they moved to Pittsburgh. Three years later they came west to Portland, a move they liked very much, especially because their parents were in Washington. Susan was born in 1953 and I in 1956.

Technically, I guess you could say Sue and I were raised Presbyterian, but we were probably closer to being just Christian. Mom taught Sunday School, and we used to attend Church on the outskirts of Portland.

As I got older we went to church less often. I had a belief in God, but I didn't see religion as an overriding influence in my life. It wasn't foremost in my mind, but generally I had the feeling that there was a higher power. It started as a child and gave me something to think about as I grew older.

Not that I was an especially spiritual person. I had good direction and went to church, but I really didn't start thinking seriously about those things until I was nineteen.

We lived in two different houses in Portland, both in what is called the West Hills area. It is a pleasant, residential section with the reputation of a place where stuck-up rich kids live. We never really thought much of it and certainly didn't think of ourselves as rich. I used to hear taunts once in a while from kids attending other schools. They'd call us "spoiled rich kids." I wasn't totally sure what they were talking about. Besides, we got respect when we played baseball because we won our games.

We were never what you'd call wealthy, but money wasn't a constant worry, either. Susan and I were well provided for. Dad had a strong sense of responsibility toward the family. We always got what we needed.

Sometimes more.

I used to get into hobbies, buying up all the books and materials I would need to get started, then drop them. I still do that more than I care to admit. I'll start something, get really interested, and go all out for a while — then just drift away from it.

I've tried about everything. I started leatherworking in sixth-grade shop class, dropped it, then picked it up again in high school. I just kind of rotate. I bought myself a guitar once and, like everyone else, thought I could teach myself to play. That lasted a couple of months.

And magic was my all-time teenage favorite! I remember thinking in high school that I wanted to be a magician. I bought all these books and . . . nothing came of it. That's how it usually happens. But I was very big on magic. My favorite trick was turning a dime into a quarter while I rubbed my hands together. That came in handy later on when I got engaged.

My urge to learn new things hasn't changed much. I've been into computers, ham radios, and sailing. I bought a sailboat and used it a couple of times, but that's all I've had a chance to do. I own a ham radio, too. A teammate of mine in the minor leagues who introduced me to the LDS church, Barry Bonnell, got me into that. It just intrigued me that I could communicate with people by using dots and dashes. I'll probably get my license and get back into it again someday.

Art is another one. It comes and goes. In the summers for about a month I'll start up—drawing, painting, that kind of thing. But I've got to take lessons and do it right because I've always sort of been in and out of wanting to be an artist.

Some of my hobbies stem from a desire to improve myself. Though I don't know much about classical music, I've been trying to develop an appreciation for it. I have a number of classical tapes that I enjoy listening to.

During 1977 spring training in West Palm Beach, Florida, I was told that the world-famous violinist Eugene Fodor was performing at a nearby concert hall. One night I was down my hotel hall and heard violin music coming from one of the rooms. Putting two and two together I decided this would be a prime opportunity to expand my knowledge of classical music with some firsthand information.

After considerable time working up the nerve, I knocked on the door. I introduced myself, told him I played for the Atlanta Braves, and explained that I was interested in his work. He was extremely gracious and invited me in. We talked for about half an hour. Then, even though his concert that night was sold out, he arranged to get me a ticket. I was thrilled.

The next day in the paper a writer referred to our meeting as a session between a classical musician and a classical catcher. At least he got one of the two right—I was hardly a classical catcher.

At the end of the 1984 season, my hobby was fly fishing. I don't know how many books I bought about it. I was really intrigued. Now I know a lot about fly fishing. I just haven't ever done it.

I don't know if you could classify dating as a hobby, though I knew guys who did, but I wasn't very proficient at it. I just wasn't a big item with the girls. I had really only one girlfriend whom I dated in high school and right up until I went into the pros after my senior year. But I didn't really date a lot. It wasn't like I had a lot of fun going to all the dances with a bunch of different girls.

I was like all high school guys; I started getting interested, but I didn't date that much. I went steady with my girlfriend until I left Portland for my second year of pro ball. I came back six months later a member of the LDS church.

Things never worked out for us. It wasn't a bad situation between us, but I came back with new feelings; I'd say, "Can't you see this Book of Mormon is true?" I just couldn't understand why everybody didn't see it. I didn't know that much about the Church then, but I knew I wanted to be married in the temple.

Until the fifth grade I played baseball looking as average or below-average as a kid can look. I certainly wasn't one of those types who was thinking about the major leagues. I was just having fun. As Mom puts it, those early baseball years "were not a *completely* disastrous experience."

Things began to change when we moved to California. I was in the fifth grade. We stayed there two years, living in Redwood City and Moraga in the Bay Area.

Willie Mays was playing for the Giants, and about then baseball became a big influence on me. Westinghouse let us use the company's box seats, so Dad would take me to the games at Candlestick Park or to Oakland to see the A's. I would sit there in the damp, cold spring nights and hope for a tie so the game would go to extra innings. We'd be freezing to death, but it didn't matter to me.

I got my first baseball glove in grade school in Portland. It had a Harvey Kuenn autograph. I greased it down and broke it in, playing with it for hours every day. But in California I got the ultimate: a Willie Mays mitt. I would watch Willie on television, study my baseball card of him, and hold my mitt just like he did. I even counted the stitches to see if there were the same number on both our gloves.

The mitt was so big it overwhelmed me, but I thought it was neat to have such a large glove. "Same thing Willie uses," I would say.

I couldn't get enough baseball. For some reason I really wanted to learn to keep score, and I still have some of the old scoresheets I kept while listening to games on the radio. Why I was so intrigued with scorekeeping, I don't know.

Our Redwood City lot was full of little rocks, and a friend and I would throw the rocks up and then bat them over the fence. We'd count each rock, and when we'd get to Babe Ruth's home-run mark we'd make this big announcement: "Dale Murphy has just broken the all-time home-run record!"

I did get to see Willie Mays in person a number of times, but I never got his autograph. Well, at least not when I was a kid. Few people knew I was a big Willie Mays fan until I got to the major leagues and was on the All-Star team in 1983. Willie was there among many former greats, and I asked for his autograph. He signed a baseball for me there in the dugout. I also got autographs from Warren Spahn, Don Drysdale, Ernie Banks, and others. I just went up and bugged them.

I don't think Willie knows he was my hero. Along with Willie, Johnny Bench was another of my heroes. When I was in high school playing catcher, Johnny was having those great years with Cincinnati. They were always my heroes, but I've never really told them so.

I'm not sure players like to hear that, because when you tell them, "Hey, you were my hero when I was a kid," they may feel a little old. In fact, I once told Sparky Lyle he had given me a baseball in Oakland when he was playing for the Boston Red Sox and I was in the sixth grade. He didn't say much, but I don't think he appreciated being reminded how long ago that was.

I met Johnny Bench for the first time in Portland, just before I was drafted in 1974. He was speaking at the Hayward Banquet, a big athletic awards dinner held every year to recognize top Oregon amateur athletes. I wasn't nominated for an award, but Jeff Dunn thought I should get some recognition. He was sitting next to Johnny, and during the dinner Jeff asked him if he would mention me because the draft was coming up. Johnny got up, introduced me, saying I was a star catcher who was going to be drafted soon, and congratulated me. I was speechless. Afterwards I thanked him for the comments, but that's about all I could get out of my mouth.

I collected a number of autographs from Giants players when I was going to games in California, but I never hung around the clubhouse door afterwards. I just went to the games and watched from afar.

While I admit I don't remember this, Dad says one night we were at Candlestick Park during a game and I said, "Dad, someday I'm going to work here."

I don't know what could have been going through my mind back then. I didn't consider myself bound for the big leagues, I'm sure of that.

Maybe I was talking about selling peanuts.

During the two years we were in California I began to improve faster. My arm was getting stronger and I did some pitching. I was nothing great with a bat, but I was finally starting to figure out what I was supposed to do.

When we moved back to Portland for my seventh grade year, I also had a strong desire to fit in with the old group — and that included making a contribution as an athlete. My parents purposely moved back to the same area of Portland — we built a new home on Richenberg Court — so we could stay with our same peer groups. I was trying harder then to prove to myself that I could compete with the Portland guys I had known before.

Shortly after we got back, basketball was on and I was all charged up about that. They didn't have school-sponsored leagues for seventh graders, but we were in the Hayhurst School area and so in the recreation league we played in, we went by the name "Hayhurst Warriors." Jeff's dad, Jack Dunn, who now coaches baseball at Portland State, would come over from Cleveland High where he was coaching and teach us basketball.

We were great. We went 46-1 in two years.

Though Mr. Dunn was a baseball coach, he knew a lot about basketball. We had a great offense with a number of different plays. Sometimes they would even give me the ball, clear everyone out, and let me go one-on-one. It was a lot of fun. We may have been the most intelligent group of eighth-graders in the country — in terms of basketball knowledge. We had presses and zone traps, and knew how to break a press.

It was all because of Mr. Dunn. He was demanding, for sure,

but we never felt he was yelling at us. He expected us to practice something and then do it. There were no complicated plays we couldn't understand, but as I look back, I can see how organized we were.

Mr. Dunn could teach. That was the great thing about him. Baseball, basketball, history — he knew how to teach concepts. He's a great coach, and we had a lot of fun because we didn't just go out there and shoot. We were better than the other teams because we practiced our plays and enjoyed it.

Mr. Dunn wanted us to do things right. He knew what he was teaching us wasn't over our heads. He would tell a lot of jokes and make us laugh, but he was serious about teaching us.

We always knew when he was mad. Mr. Dunn always wore wingtips, and if we weren't doing things right, his foot would be slamming down on the ground — WHAM! WHAM! He would never yell at us. He wasn't interested in hurting our feelings. He'd just slam those wingtips.

I was now taking sports more seriously and was determined to do things right — whether my knobby-kneed body was willing to comply or not. But the furthest I dared dream was making the high school baseball team. I would watch them play and say, "I sure hope I can do that someday." That was my goal, to play Wilson High baseball. That to me was the major leagues. I set my sights on that, thinking it would be outstanding if I could ever advance that far.

Meanwhile, I was getting pretty good in basketball. I was scoring a lot of points on the Hayhurst team. I prided myself on keeping my head and staying cool because of my dislike for confrontations.

But when I got to high school I started yelling at the refs. I don't know why that happened.

It was out of frustration, I guess. In the seventh and eighth grades I was good and scored a lot of points. I was able to keep up. But in high school I slowed down. I grew taller fast and slowed down on my feet; I began to foul a lot because I couldn't keep up with some of the others.

When a foul was called on me (I maintain a basketball referee's job is the toughest in sports because he can't always see the play), I'd get mad. I went through a period when the way I was acting surprised even me.

Not being the top scorer didn't bother me. Our team was known for good defense, and during my senior year we got our first state tournament win in the school's history. I liked to set up plays and throw good passes. After I was moved from the post to point guard, we went 14-1. I was really happy about my situation on the team.

I never complained in baseball. If I was out, I was out. I never have been able to understand why I'd lose control in basketball. Every once in a while I still see a guy in Portland who once called two technicals on me in a game. We just laugh about it.

It wasn't so humorous then.

I could keep up in baseball, even though I wasn't fast, because I could hit and throw. If a player can do those things, he can hold his own, so I didn't really have many problems there. But in basketball I was just being outmanuevered; it was frustrating because in the seventh and eighth grades it hadn't been that way.

About my sophomore year a growth spurt pushed me up to six-three or six-four and I slowed down even more. The harder I tried to keep up, the more I fouled. But I still managed to play well enough to get a lot of playing time.

My senior year, 1974, we went 20-8 and 2-2 in the state tournament. I made second team all-city, though averaging only 9.5 points a game.

I also got a technical foul during one of the tournament games.

By the end of my high school basketball career, though, I must have mellowed out a little, because I was voted Most Inspirational Player on the team. I had things under control.

Sort of.

3 Signing Up

Catching, the position that became my ticket into professional baseball, was never a big consideration until I was thirteen. My summer league coach asked me if I wanted to catch for the last couple of innings one game and I said sure.

My arm was pretty strong and people were starting to notice. Until I got into American Legion baseball in the ninth grade my plan was just to play—anywhere and as much as possible. But after trying the position out a few times, I knew I liked catching just fine.

Mr. Dunn, who coached our Legion team and had also moved over from Cleveland High to coach the Wilson High team, somehow got the idea when I was a freshman that I might have a future in the sport as a catcher. My arm made me a natural for that or for pitching, and I am grateful I never pitched that much. Too many kids hurt their arms by pitching a lot at a young age.

I did have my moments on the mound. When playing once in California, I had a Sandy Koufax–type day. We played six-inning games and by the last inning I had struck out all seventeen players and there were two outs. I walked a guy and he stole second base. Our catcher — thinking I wanted to strike out every man we put out — didn't even throw the ball on the steal.

I was really upset. He was trying to do me a favor, but I was mad he didn't try to get the guy. Anyway, another batter came up and flew out to end my streak.

I had a good arm, but as I got older I couldn't get guys out. It was weird. They'd still hit off me. Maybe they put me behind the plate because I was never really that successful in my early teens as a pitcher.

Things began to escalate once I was in the ninth grade at Wilson High. Susan was a senior, and even though I was sort of a pest around her, she looked out for me. People started talking to her about what I was doing on the baseball field — something she wasn't used to — but she never seemed to resent it.

Football was a sport I liked. Most of my friends went out for freshman football, but I didn't want to play. I didn't want to get hurt and had the idea that the game was dangerous.

Susan's social studies teacher was also the freshman football coach, and he was trying to get me to play. He'd frequently suggest to her that I really ought to come out. One day she got tired of it and told him, "Keep your hands off him."

Like I said, she looked out for me.

Ironically, that year I sustained my first baseball injury: a broken thumb on my right hand. After the x-rays and preliminary work, the doctor began to cast it. When he was done he asked, "How does that feel?"

I told him it felt fine but he had put the cast on the wrong hand.

Until the end of my sophomore year, it had never dawned on me that I might have a chance to make a living playing baseball. My dad and Mr. Dunn had been talking a little about it, so I started to get the picture. From talking with Mr. Dunn about the pro scouts attending the games, I knew I was being watched. I started thinking about what might happen. I began thinking that maybe I should start taking this seriously. Mr. Dunn told me that as a freshman they had judged my abilities as above average. The scouts started to appear in my sophomore year; by the time I was a junior we were considering the possibilities of my becoming a pro player, and as a senior we began thinking about a signing bonus.

My arm got most of the attention. I was hitting home runs

and batting .400 — but a lot of guys do that in high school. They weren't interested in me for my hitting, even though I had a lot of good nights at the plate, especially my last year or two of Legion ball. One night we were playing a team from the Kelso-Longview, Washington, area. The wind was blowing in from center field at about thirty-five miles an hour. I smashed one straight over the center-field fence. An old timer next to Mr. Dunn said he had been watching baseball there for years and had never seen one hit that far over that fence, let alone against the wind.

All things considered, though, they figured I was only an average batter who could learn to hit. That can be taught. But the arm was something I was born with.

In high school baseball my school was always tough but never could win the state championship. We'd get to the quarterfinals or semifinals, lose a close one, and end up gearing for Legion play. Jeff and John Dunn and Bruce Plato were close friends of mine and played on the high school and Legion teams with me. We won three straight Portland Interscholastic League titles but couldn't get through the state tourney. We'd play about twenty games and never quite jell until we got to Legion.

In Legion we were awesome.

Our coach, Mr. Dunn, had a great philosophy. He said, "You guys can have a job and not play baseball and that's fine. But if you play baseball I want you to be at practice every morning, so it will be hard to do both a job and baseball." He told us that what we learned in baseball would help us, maybe even earn us a college scholarship. But even if we didn't get a scholarship, he continued, we would learn things that would help us after high school. "So you can make your investment here or you can get a job."

He didn't stop kids from working as much as he had a system that almost required us to be free from other obligations. What he said about his program helping us later in life was true. I learned things there that I haven't been taught even in professional baseball.

So in the summers, all we did was play baseball. I became very dedicated. I'd drill holes in my bats, fill them with lead, and practice swinging them by the hour in the basement. Mom says I was "the height of dedication" when it came to sports. (I was something less than that when it came to chores.)

Mr. Dunn and Roy Love — now athletic director at Portland State — directed a summer baseball camp for Little Leaguers, and once we were out of school, Jeff, John, and I helped out there. We played so much baseball we couldn't help but get better. We practiced with our Legion team for two hours every morning, followed by the day camp. It was the only job I ever had, and I worked there for three hours a day. Then we went home to rest for a couple of hours before batting practice and a Legion game.

We'd do that almost every day.

In 1972 — after my sophomore year in high school — we missed a chance to go to the nationals when a team from Lewiston (Idaho)–Clarkston (Washington) beat us in the championship game. One of their players hit a single with the bases loaded and two outs in the last of the ninth inning.

The following year we won the regionals and went to the Legion World Series in Lewiston. We should have won it all. We beat defending champion Cincinnati but ended up losing games to Puerto Rico and Memphis. We finished the year third in the Series and with an overall 54-8 record.

I didn't get to finish out the next season. Things were interrupted when I was drafted by the Braves.

My first serious baseball injury came during my sophomore year. It made me realize that baseball doesn't last forever.

I was catching in a game, and my shin guards were a little too small. They didn't quite cover my knees, and I was catching for Gail Meier — the hardest thrower on our pitching staff. A guy foul-tipped a pitch, and the ball caught me right on the kneecap above the protective guard. I walked around a minute thinking, "Hey, that hurts pretty good."

It didn't go away. Not that game. Not that season. I just kept playing on it all summer, trying to work the soreness out. At first I thought it would kill me, but I just kept going.

My junior year of high school was starting, and it wasn't getting any better. One night I climbed some stairs ahead of Dad; he noticed my pantleg hanging loose on one side and the other stretching tight around my knee. My bad leg had atrophied to the point where he could see the difference. We decided to get it checked.

One doctor x-rayed it and told us there was not a loose bone fragment, so there wasn't a need to operate. He did suggest that I should stop catching. I was stunned. About that time I was starting to realize I might have a chance to play pro baseball, and I felt my only shot was as a catcher. We were pretty upset.

The doctor didn't tell me to quit baseball, just to quit catching. The way I had it figured, they were the same thing.

We consulted another doctor who knew something about baseball. He pointed out that Johnny Bench wasn't six-foot-four like me, and maybe I ought to change positions anyway. I was thinking, "Gosh, this is just great."

My parents and I finally decided to go down to Eugene, Oregon, to see a Dr. Don Slocum. He had been a pioneer in treating sports injuries and had a good reputation.

After he examined the x-rays he said, "We have to operate." The other doctors hadn't wanted to operate, since the fragment wasn't floating loose. Dr. Slocum said it wouldn't get any better, adding, "If I operate, it will either stay the same or get better, so you have a better chance of recovering if I operate."

We were all in favor of that. I just didn't realize until after it was all over how serious it was. The cracked part of my kneecap was near the tendon connection. They had to cut the tendon, remove the chip, drill holes in the kneecap, and sew the tendon back to it.

Consequently, I missed playing basketball my junior season. Considering my reputation with the refs, it was probably just as well.

By spring I was ready to go, regardless of the objections my knee put up. I tried to catch too soon and got tendinitis. I ended up playing first base in high school, but finally, when Legion started, I went back to full-time catching.

The last few months before the draft were kind of hectic. Scouts checked me out at every game. Several said I couldn't hit. Mr. Dunn and Roy Love did most of the talking to scouts to keep the pressure off us, but my family couldn't avoid becoming involved. As Susan would be watching the games, a scout would appear, buy her a hot dog and a soft drink, and then quiz her on me — how was the knee? was I going to college? — anything they could get from her. There was so much talk in the stands about where I should be playing or what I should be doing that Mom finally retreated behind the center-field fence and watched the games from there.

I was having a great year. My knee was fine. But I had more on my mind than my knee that spring. A lot more.

Early on I hoped that my baseball might get me a college scholarship. I wanted to attend college, so naturally I started looking at schools with good baseball programs.

At first I was a little nervous about playing pro ball. If it works out, fine, I thought. But playing college ball and earning a scholarship was also one of my goals.

I started getting asked to tryout camps just before the draft. The Phillies flew me to Philadelphia, which was really exciting. Although I had known the scouts were watching me, I didn't think anyone really might want to draft me. It still seemed too unrealistic. I was planning on going to college on scholarship; I just wanted to keep playing baseball.

I leaned towards Arizona State because of its baseball program. (If I had gone there I would have played on the same team with Bob Horner.) Several friends went to Portland State, Oregon State, or Oregon, but I made a visit to ASU.

Those schools were about the only ones really interested. There weren't that many colleges interested in me, anyway. I think Stanford contacted me, though I don't know if my grades were good enough. I wasn't one of those guys saying, "Well, let's see, which college am I going to visit this week?"

So other than the Oregon schools I visited only one—ASU. I signed a letter of intent to go there.

Then the Atlanta Braves drafted me—number one.

Dad and I hadn't really dissected the issue until the draft. Then we thought, let's try and put a dollar value on how much a professional team would have to pay to persuade us to miss four or five years of school. We figured that if I didn't make it after five years, I'd just go back to school.

The Braves set up a meeting with us in a Portland hotel. I was just out of high school and didn't know much of anything. Dad was my agent and we negotiated the contract together.

A little negotiating work took place but nothing really high-powered. We met with Bill Wight, the Braves' West Coast scout, and talked it over.

When they hesitated at the bonus we wanted I said, "Well, hey, I don't have to sign. I'm going to college." I thought I was driving a pretty hard bargain. Of course, the only leverage I had in that situation was that I could go to ASU, a premier baseball school.

That didn't faze Bill. He just answered, "You're only going there to play baseball. You know you're not going there to get an education."

Maybe he was right, but we worked it out anyway. We got the figures we were looking for. The offer was just over $50,000. There it was. What now? Was I going to take it or not?

Once we reached the point during the discussions that the money was right, my parents just looked at me and said, "It's your decision."

"I think I'm gonna try it," I said.

It ended up being a lot of fun even though we really didn't know what we were getting into, but we were proud of ourselves. After I signed, we walked outside. I don't know how much money Dad was making then, but that was a lot of money to both of us. We just looked at each other and started laughing. "You know how much money that is?" he said.

I didn't, but it sounded good.

We opened an account in the bank the next day to deposit the bonus money. We put it in Mom's name. I had no idea what to do with that much money.

Really it wasn't too difficult a decision. I had my parents' support, always quiet and reassuring and trusting. And I had the big bonus. (In the lower rounds of the draft, the money's not there. They may only offer $1,000 to sign, and that's when the decisions get tough.)

I had the bonus and I knew it was something I wanted to try. But money had never been a big objective with me. I probably would have signed even if the money hadn't been right. It sounded so intriguing. But even then I had no idea that I would get a shot at the major leagues. No idea at all.

I told Bill Wight I had one more thing to take care of. I wanted to play in one last Legion game with the guys. Bill didn't like it. He grimaced and told me that if I got hurt everything was off.

My friends and I weren't a particularly sentimental group; we relied mainly on jokes or pranks to get the message across. But I wasn't going to miss the chance to say good-bye to them.

The last game was a sweet one. I hit a home run.

4 Minor Leagues, Major Changes

As the plane lifted out of Portland and turned east, it began to sink in just how far from home I was going. The Braves had assigned me for the 1974 season to a rookie league team in Kingsport, Tennessee, which consisted mainly of recently signed high school and college players. Rookie league is the first and lowest level of minor league baseball, the first chance to sample playing the game for money and living the life-style of a pro athlete.

It was pretty glamorous . . . for the first day. Bill Lucas, the director of player development, met me in Atlanta and took me to a hotel for the night, one of the fancy ones in the city. The next morning I caught a flight to Kingsport.

When I joined the team it seemed everyone knew at least one thing about me: I'd been the top draft choice. I'd enter the clubhouse and they would call out, "Hey Number One!" They were just teasing me, but it made me feel a little self-conscious, knowing Atlanta had paid me big money to make good in their organization.

But I found out early that pro baseball, especially in the minors, isn't really glamorous after all. They issued my uniform. Instead of the tight-fitting double-knits I had worn in high school, it was an old wool thing the Atlanta Braves had used maybe seven or eight years earlier.

The ball field was—I would learn later—as good as could be expected at that level, but then they don't have all the money in the world to take care of things.

It didn't take long to miss the comforts of home. I stayed in a motel room that first summer with an infielder named Steve Oliva and later with pitcher Joey McLaughlin. We got around $500 a month and $5 a day meal money. A bus took us to our games.

That first day I asked myself, "So this is pro ball, huh?"

I called home a lot. The local people were gracious, but Kingsport wasn't home and I wasn't playing baseball with my friends from Portland. I was lonely and a little homesick.

It was the longest year of my career. I was just trying to survive the season and get back home. I wasn't thinking about major league baseball or even planning to have a really great year so I could move up. I just wanted to survive.

One morning after a workout at the Kingsport field, I started feeling sick. The manager told me to go take a rest. I went back to the motel and crawled in bed. I missed the sympathy I would get at home and, in fact, the most sympathy I did get was when I called back to Portland and talked to Mom.

While the uniforms and ballparks weren't too impressive, the competition was. That was another matter entirely. I was straight out of high school; most of the others had played college ball. Everybody on the field had been on an all-star team or hit .400. When you turn pro, high school stats don't mean much.

Sometimes I felt I was in over my head. I was impressed even then with Lance Parrish (now with Detroit), who was playing for Bristol, and Butch Wynegar (now with the New York Yankees), another catcher, playing for Elizabethton. I knew back then those guys were going to make it.

That first jump, from high school to pro baseball, is one of the biggest a player has to make. All of a sudden everybody is good at something. Everyone can throw hard or hit the ball a long way.

You are adjusting to being away from home, the life-style of pro baseball, and learning the game as you go. You find it hard to hit because the pitchers don't have much control; you never know where the ball will be coming. Lights aren't good and travel is new, so you face a lot of distractions. If you make it in rookie league ball, you've done a lot.

A player normally progresses from rookie to Class A, to Double A, Triple A, and finally to the major leagues. Perhaps the other most difficult step is from Class A to Double A. You find yourself thrown in with guys who have been in the big leagues. You start facing pitchers who have good control and good stuff; but the lights still aren't that good, so it becomes more difficult to hit.

Tough as the minor leagues are, they are also fun. There is a certain closeness with the players that you kind of miss in the majors. It's a learning, growing experience. You're all just trying to get by and all making about the same kind of money. If you're married, you probably just got married, and that's an adjustment, too. It's all kind of new.

My first manager in Kingsport was former major-league knuckleball artist Hoyt Wilhelm. He was easygoing and laid-back, even when we didn't play well. One night after we had lost six straight games, a player said, "Don't worry, Hoyt; it's only a matter of time before we start playing well."

"Yeah, I know," said Hoyt with a slow grin, "but we're running out of time."

Once in a while at the end of batting practice, when some of us were getting cocky, Hoyt would throw us a few of the knucklers he was famous for. None of us had ever seen a real knuckler, and none of us could hit Hoyt's. We were no match.

I was catching well, which seemed to keep the right people interested. One newspaper quoted Hoyt as saying I was the best catcher he'd ever seen and would be in the majors in three years. My hitting wasn't impressive; nobody saw me as a big threat at the plate. I did hit five home runs during that first season of seventy-one games. Two of those came during the same week; after that I didn't think they'd ever get me out again. I finished with a .254 batting average and even made the all-star team, which shows you don't have to be a big hitter to become an all-star in rookie league. It was my defensive ability that got me drafted and that's what kept me there.

I ended the year feeling that it had been lonely and strange at times, but that I had enjoyed it. I was happy, though, when it was time to return home again to Portland.

After spring training in 1975 I was assigned to Greenwood, South Carolina, the Braves' Class A team in the Western Carolinas League. It was a big change if for no other reason than the extended schedule. Instead of 71 games, we played 140; finishing out a season that long can become a test of endurance.

But things were starting to look up. In Kingsport we hung our clothes on two hooks on the clubhouse wall. In Greenwood we had our own lockers. Instead of living in a motel, I rented a house with two other players just outside town. The increase in space alone made things better.

There were a lot of nice people in Greenwood. Following afternoon games, the townspeople would put on a big buffet for the players underneath the stands. Sometimes they would leave bags of fruit or vegetables on our doorstep.

While living conditions improved, my hitting didn't. I got only five home runs all year, despite playing twice as many games.

My start — not to mention the team's start — was not impressive. After the first thirteen games I was hitting just .204 with no home runs and only four runs batted in. We were 5-8. At mid-May I was still hitting only .200 with just 10 RBI. I was already starting to envision future newspaper stories: *Light-hitting catcher Dale Murphy surprised everyone by rapping a two-out triple to left field . . .*

By June I wasn't much better, though our manager, Bobby Dews, didn't say anything to me about being dissatisfied. I had only two home runs and was hitting just .220; in one string we lost fifteen of sixteen games. One night Bobby replaced me as catcher with Ron Rockhill and he hit a two-run home run, which didn't make me feel any more confident about my hitting.

There was one bright spot that year. We acquired outfielder Barry Bonnell from the Philadelphia organization; he had a reputation around the league as a hot prospect. He and I hit next to each other in the lineup. I use the term "hit" loosely, because his average was around 100 percentage points better than mine most of the year.

Barry was playing center field and having his way at the plate. He was knocking in runs and batting around .325. The manager told reporters he was planning on disconnecting Barry's phone so the Braves wouldn't call him up to a higher level. (Bobby also told them he needed more hitting from people like . . . um . . . Dale Murphy.) Barry was the only player on the team to hit over .300 the first half of the season.

At year's end, Barry and I both made the all-star team. I had a clear idea why he made it. In my case the reason why wasn't so clear. Barry hit .319 with 12 home runs and 80 RBI. I hit 5 home runs, had a .231 average with 50 RBI. We didn't make the playoffs.

Despite my hitting, they kept telling me my catching was fine, and that was more important. The Braves told me I was progressing on schedule.

I started seeing people who were going places the next year (1976) when I was assigned to Savannah, the Double-A affiliate of the Southern League.

Two players that impressed me most were Eddie Murray, playing for Charlotte, and Willie Wilson of Jacksonville. Of course, both went on to become stars in the big leagues, Eddie for Baltimore and Willie at Kansas City. Eddie would come up to the plate switch-hitting and slamming home runs.

Willie wasn't a completely new face to me. Just before I was drafted, Willie and I flew out to Philadelphia so they could take a look at us. They lined the players up to time us in a 60-yard dash, looked over to me and another guy, and said, "Okay, you two run." I was up against Willie Wilson. Needless to say, I didn't beat him.

Over the course of that season in Savannah, he stole a lot of bases on me. Although I don't recall the situation, I remember I managed to throw him out one time: even catching him once was enough to stick in my memory.

I had made the adjustment to Double-A baseball well enough. I was still young and throwing well. People all around me were hitting farther and for better averages, but the Braves kept telling me I was doing fine—and I kept making the all-star teams.

My first night in Savannah I got a hit in three at-bats, which may not seem spectacular, but I hadn't seen a .300 batting average beside my name more than once or twice since I had turned pro.

Things were looking good, particularly when I noted that the left-field wall was only 290 feet down the third base line. A right-handed hitter, I figured this was my chance to park a few.

But I hadn't taken the pitching into consideration, I guess. I ended up hitting twelve home runs that year and only two of them went over the short left-field wall.

During that summer I started to put on weight and gain strength. And though I wasn't getting that many hits, the press clippings piled up. Writers were referring to me as a "can't miss" prospect. A story in a Savannah paper said I had a "bionic arm" and quoted an Atlanta official as saying I had the best arm in baseball.

Luckily, he wasn't asked to rate my hitting.

Our manager was the late Tommie Aaron, brother of the home-run king Henry and a veteran major leaguer himself. Tommie was popular with the players, always wearing a big smile and obviously enjoying the games. He never got too uptight. One of the things he told us was that we should develop "the strength to be calm."

That took some doing, especially on his part. We ended the season 69-71.

I hit .267 in Savannah with twelve home runs and was called up to Triple-A Richmond for eighteen games at the end of the year, where I hit four more home runs and batted .260.

That first trip to Richmond was a little strange. I cost us the playoffs with a bad throw, the beginning of a throwing problem that could have ended my career. I came moping into the clubhouse after that loss, and someone told me the manager, Jack McKeon, wanted to see me.

I figured I deserved what I was going to get, having cost us the game. But I didn't get chewed out after all. He told me I was being called up to the major leagues.

5   "The Bigs"

I got to Los Angeles on a Saturday night to join the Braves in a series against the Dodgers, but it rained all day Sunday and they had to postpone the game. They scheduled us for a 10:00 A.M. Monday game at Dodger Stadium.

It was late in the season, and the Braves were already out of the pennant race. It was the time when the big-league teams call up their prospects and look at them under major-league conditions, planning their moves for future years.

I was nervous all weekend and got up early for breakfast on Monday. Everybody, including a pitcher named Jamie Easterly who had been called up when I was, congregated in the lobby.

Dave Bristol, then the Braves' manager, pulled me aside just before we left for the ballpark. "Hey, you're gonna catch the second game. Just go out there and don't worry. There's no difference between this park and any of those you've been playing in. Oh, it's got a few more people in the stands [very few, it turned out], but just play your game and you won't have any problems. You'll be fine."

The clubhouse wasn't an entirely unfamiliar scene. I hadn't been in Dodger Stadium, but having been to spring training the past two years, I knew most of the Braves' players. Several came over and offered encouragement.

It helped some, but it didn't stop me from being scared.

Not that there was any roaring crowd to contend with. Only 6,559 came to the game, the smallest in Dodger Stadium history. I sat in the dugout through the first game of the double-header and got my call in the second game.

Jamie Easterly was pitching for us, and right off I started having some throwing troubles. The Dodgers stole three bases off me, two by Davey Lopes and one by Bill Russell. I didn't throw anything into the outfield, I just didn't get the ball to second base in time.

Rick Rhoden was pitching for the Dodgers. When it was my turn to bat, I went up to the plate telling myself all the while to just relax. I let the first pitch go by and said to myself, "Boy, I maybe could have hit that." I guess the reality of the situation started to set in. The pitch I had seen wasn't actually unhittable.

I ended up with two hits in four at-bats in my first major-league game. The first one was something of a fluke. Rhoden threw me a slider on the outside edge of the plate, and I swung and kind of topped the ball down the third base line. We had a runner on third, and L.A.'s third baseman, Ron Cey, came charging in. He quickly snapped the ball toward first, but Steve Garvey had to pull his foot off the bag as he stretched to catch it.

The official scorer was kind. He ruled it a hit, deciding I had beaten the throw anyway; and the runner scored from third, giving me a hit and an RBI.

I walked back to first base after the hit, and there, standing right next to me, was Steve Garvey, one of baseball's best players. My mind was a blank. I was thinking, "What am I going to say now? I'm standing right next to Steve Garvey." He spared me further anxiety, saying, "Congratulations, Dale. I hope you get many more."

Steve didn't even know who I was, other than just another kid who had been called up at the end of the season, but his acknowledging the hit was a big deal to me. I had proven I could hit major-league pitching and could even talk with Steve Garvey (though my response to him consisted of a mumbled "Thanks").

They gave me the ball as a memento.

During the last couple of weeks of that season I had other thrills. In the next-to-last game Phil Niekro, Atlanta's legendary knuckleball pitcher, came close to throwing a no-hitter with me behind the plate. I fretted the whole game about being charged with passed balls or a throwing error or generally messing up his big chance. Phil was the epitome of patience. He didn't seem to be bothered by a nervous rookie trying to catch his pitches. I had four passed balls that game.

It got around to the ninth inning and I was trying to calm myself down. You would have thought *I* was throwing the no-hitter. Tommie Aaron's admonition to "have the strength to be calm" was firmly fixed in my mind, but it wasn't working too well.

Cincinnati's Cesar Geronimo came to the plate with one out. Phil threw the knuckler — a decent one — and Geronimo doubled down the left field line.

I was dejected. I had come close to catching a no-hitter. I don't remember ever being more disappointed about a game.

In that season-ending series against Cincinnati, I was trying to prove something. I wanted my first big-league home run. I kept trying and trying . . . too hard. I got into the batter's box in one of the games and faced the Reds' Don Gullett. He could throw as hard as anybody I'd ever seen. He could also throw a forkball, something I'd *never* seen.

As I was getting set up in the box, I heard a whistle from the Reds' dugout. Johnny Bench was catching, and when I looked over that way, I saw their manager, Sparky Anderson, call, "Hey, Johnny!" He then motioned with his hands to have Gullett throw the ball up and inside. He wanted to see if I could hit a high tight one, often a trouble pitch for big players.

I hit the next pitch to the warning track and the left fielder hauled it in, but even coming close did me good. At least now Sparky and I both knew I could hit that inside fastball.

During that last series it started to really sink in that I was in the major leagues, that someday I might stay there. But I was still having trouble believing what was going on. I'd look out on the field and see them: George Foster, Johnny Bench, Pete Rose.

Those guys were baseball legends.

And I was playing with them.

6 A Different Kind of Contract

During spring training in West Palm Beach, Florida, in 1975, I was sitting at the dinner table with several other players when someone brought up the subject of the Bible.

Religion had been part of my upbringing and I had always felt there was a higher power of some type, but that was about the depth of my spiritual insight. I had never really pursued things much further. I had been christened in a Presbyterian church as a baby and attended some church in Portland when I was young, but I really didn't have a background in the scriptures. At least not enough to take part in that dinner-time conversation with the players. But being away from home and alone, with a lot of time to think, I found that those things began to interest me.

I listened closely to what they were saying. Somebody said there was a new translation of the Bible out, written in terms that "modern man" could understand. He said you could read it and it would make sense. I was too unsure to join in the conversation, so I just sat there in a rather noncommittal way. At that stage, I had no idea if it was going to be just another of my interests that turns into a hobby, only to be forgotten.

Their talk about a need for religion seemed to make sense, and I started reading the Bible and any pamphlets I could get hold of. I began to feel that religion was something I would like to become involved in.

During that time I came in contact with others who said they had found Christ. They told me about God and accepting Christ. I started to feel good about my plans to make some changes in my life. But they were only general changes. Being a better person, living a more spiritually centered life, things like that. I really had no direction.

A fellow from Athletes in Action gave me a tract listing the steps to being born again. It involved confessing you are a sinner, saying you are sorry, asking the Lord to enter your life, and being born again. It sounded good. I was trying, gradually, to make such changes, and I started to read the Bible even more and attend whatever church services I could.

Dad was visiting me in Florida that spring and one day I asked him if he would like to attend an Easter sunrise service the next Sunday. He said he would, though I'm sure he was surprised. He had never known me to initiate church attendance.

I began to tell other players and a few friends that I was going to change. Some encouraged me and others told me to steer clear of that stuff—they said it was too strange. I was trying to stop drinking, change my views on morality, and just live a more spiritual existence.

How to do it was another matter.

Something told me I needed to change my life, but I didn't really have any guidance. My belief and my faith were vague. I felt good about the changes I was trying to make, but had no specific plan. I didn't know how to pray, or if I was supposed to, or where to go to church, or even if that was important.

There were so many questions. Even on drinking there was a lot of debate. Some said it was okay to drink a beer, that it wasn't a big deal; others said I should quit. It was so confusing. Though I had the feeling I was headed in the right direction, I didn't know my destination or how to tell when I had arrived.

The Braves assigned me to Greenwood, South Carolina, that spring, and when I got there I attended a church a couple of times, but didn't seem to find many answers. During the season there was a trade with the Phillies, and a talented young outfielder named Barry Bonnell came to Greenwood to play.

I knew Barry would help the club. His stats showed that. But

I had no idea just how much he would help me in other, far more important ways.

Though I didn't know it at the time, Barry was a Mormon, a member of The Church of Jesus Christ of Latter-day Saints. The only Mormon I had ever known in school was Ernie Thompson, a baseball teammate in Oregon.

Ernie was a great guy. Everybody liked him. Looking back, I guess there was something different about him. He was the only player in the group who could have said "Hey, I love you guys," and not have everybody laugh at him.

I remembered that after he got out of high school Ernie said he was going to Brigham Young University in Utah. He said it was a school owned by the church he belonged to. Later I heard he was going on what he called a "mission" in some foreign country for his church.

That was all I knew about Mormons.

Then came Barry. There was always something honest and sincere about him. I hit it off with him well from the start.

Several other times players brought up religion and I found myself listening intently. I never said much because I was quite timid about what I was doing, but soon I found I was interested, actively interested, in finding out who I was.

It was near midnight when I clambered onto the team bus. There was nothing to look forward to except an eight-hour bus ride in the dark from Rocky Mount, North Carolina, to Greenwood. The players climbed on, one or two at a time, carrying their gear as they went.

I slipped into a window seat, not expecting to sleep much. Nobody slept much on the old school-bus bench seats. Usually I just sat there and stared out of the window into the darkness, doing a lot of thinking or slipping in and out of a doze.

Barry was different from the ordinary ballplayer. Often the team members would goof around in the back or read men's magazines on the road swings, but I noticed Barry wasn't involved in that. He was always reading this book with a blue cover.

I learned that Barry was a Mormon, and that the blue book he packed around was called the Book of Mormon. He used to read it at night on the bus, holding a flashlight so he could see. Players would think he was looking at something really titillating. They would come up and ask, "Hey, Barry, whadaya reading?"

He would tell them. Then they'd go immediately back to their seats, some of them shaking their heads as they went.

One day I told him, "Barry, I'm trying to make some changes in my life."

"That's a good thing. It's something right to do," he said.

That night Barry sat in the seat next to me. We waited in silence for a few minutes as the bus rumbled past the street lights and out of town.

Barry started talking generally about religion, and I mentioned again that I was trying to change. He was very supportive, saying that it was great. Soon we were deep in conversation, the miles rolling by unnoticed. I wasn't paying attention to where we were. What Barry was saying to me sounded good. It sounded right, and I was feeling an impression that it was true. I could feel the Spirit strongly, although I didn't know that's what it was at the time.

Barry asked me if I had been baptized. I told him no (later on I found I had been christened as a child). "I didn't know baptism was something important to do," I said.

He told me it was very important, that it was something I needed to do. He explained that the Savior was baptized to set an example for us. I said it sounded right and put it in the back of my mind.

He brought up the subject of prophets, saying in his search for the truth he had studied a lot of religions and had wondered why nobody believed in prophets today. Why wasn't there a Moses or an Abraham now to tell us what the Lord wants?

I didn't really know what he was talking about, because I didn't know who Abraham and Moses were, other than a few vague recollections of the names from my past church activities in Portland.

He continued, saying he had wondered why there was no prophet today. Then he said he had discovered there is one.

I was intrigued. I asked Barry who it was, and he told me this prophet's name was Spencer W. Kimball.

That impressed me. He knew about a prophet and he knew his name. I thought it was kind of special.

I thought suddenly about Ernie Thompson from Oregon. I mentioned him and his mission, and Barry said, "Oh yeah, we have missionaries all over the world."

The discussion went on into the night.

Our bus pulled into Greenwood shortly after sunrise. We got off and Barry said, "Dale, do you feel good about what we've talked about?"

We'd covered a lot of territory. Barry said later that he had told me everything he knew about the Church. He'd been a member only a couple of years.

I told him I felt great about what we had discussed, that some of the things sounded really wonderful. I said I felt as if I had received a blessing.

Our conversation was on my mind almost constantly for the next couple of days. Then Barry approached me again: "Dale, you know the things we discussed on the bus the other night? Would you like to know more about it?"

I said I would.

Barry and the Elders came to my apartment the next night. I was excited, but nervous. When we started talking about the Church the Elders would bring up something involving the gospel and ask if I'd ever heard it before.

"No."

Barry would laugh. "What are you talking about? I told you that the other night on the bus," he'd say.

Like I said, I was nervous. I was also slightly confused, but it continued to sound good. It wasn't in one all-encompassing instant that I felt this was the truth. Rather, it was a constant assurance that I was being taught the truth.

That first missionary discussion left me very emotionally moved. I just walked around my house for hours, thinking about what they had said. It was true. I knew it.

They had talked about Joseph Smith and the need for living prophets. As I walked around I found myself crying as I thought about it. I didn't really know why. Why was I like that? I liked what I had heard and at the same time I knew there would be conflicts, changes.

I felt I had been taught something really good. I may not have had a full testimony that first night, but I did know it was right and that it was going to require some commitment. I wasn't sure how those changes were going to be met by my family and friends.

For days I continued to think about what had been said. One afternoon I found myself out just driving around, going nowhere in particular. I passed a church — it wasn't a Mormon meetinghouse—and pulled over and went in. I couldn't get the things I had been studying off my mind. Inside, I sat down and began praying like I had never prayed before—praying for help and direction and strength, praying that I would do what the Lord wanted me to do.

The Elders told me to read a certain passage in the Book of Mormon: Moroni 10:3–5. They said to read it and ask myself if any man could have written the Book of Mormon or if it was inspired by the Lord. I started praying after that first discussion and continued to pray and study. The more I read and talked to the Bonnells and the missionaries, the more sure I felt. They were explaining things that made a lot of sense to me.

I started attending church and continued the discussions. Because of my road trips, it took me a couple of months to get through the discussions. During that time I would go to church and feel so uplifted. I was finding the direction I had been looking for in those initial commitments I had made.

The missionaries—Elders Ron Neilsen and Brian Miller—influenced me a great deal. I knew what a special commitment they had made at that time in their lives. I looked at the way Barry and Stefnie were living, and it was exciting to me.

Even before I was baptized a member of the Church, I started to go tracting with the Elders. We'd take turns giving door approaches and then buy ice cream for the one who placed the most copies of the Book of Mormon in homes. I'd go up and knock on a door and say, "We have a message about Jesus Christ," and ask if they were interested.

All this while the Church so involved my thinking that I was having some trouble at the plate. I didn't seem to be concentrating too well on baseball. One Sunday at church in Greenwood, Brother Ralph Yingling came up to me and asked, "Are you all right? You look a little confused about things."

He gave me a blessing, which made me feel confident and sure I was doing the right things. Things began to get better.

A few days later during one of the lessons the Elders kind of surprised me. They asked me if I wanted to be baptized. I hadn't planned on being asked that question so soon, but when it came all I said was, "Yes."

I was really excited. I didn't jump up and down physically, but in my mind I was jumping for joy. I was saying to myself, "I'm going to be baptized!" and that was a great thing to me. It was the most important thing I could do.

Meanwhile, the missionaries were jumping up and down. Physically.

The next step was a big one: telling everyone. I put it off as long as possible.

I waited until the night before my baptism to call my parents. I was nervous and didn't know how they would react. After all, it was a major change for me. I was just nineteen years old, and I wasn't sure how people who were important to me would feel about what I was doing. But I knew the Lord had shown me the truth.

When I got on the phone, I told my parents I had been studying a few things and that I was going to join the Mormon church — the next day.

Both were very understanding. Dad wasn't extremely surprised, having been with me in spring training and seen my interest in religion. He had worked with a number of Mormons — something I hadn't known before — and told me he respected them.

Dad told me to be true to what I believed, and then asked me to take part in a test with him to make sure I was doing the right thing.

"Son, I'm going to play devil's advocate here. I'm going to think of any negative things I can about the LDS church and present them to you as reasons not to join when we talk on the phone tomorrow. We can see if this is really what you want."

I agreed.

The call came the next day. My dad came on the line and said, "Dale, I tried to think of some reasons why you shouldn't join the Mormon church, and I . . . well, I couldn't think of any. If you think this is right, we're both behind you a thousand percent."

Barry baptized me the day after the season ended in an LDS meetinghouse in Greenwood. Afterwards I was confirmed by Elder Miller, who said in the blessing that I would marry in the temple.

During my conversion process I had come up with some questions, as all investigators do, but the Spirit kept telling me to keep going. The feeling that this was right was always there.

Explaining that feeling to people back in Portland was difficult. I got the full support of my family, although Sue had some reservations at first. The Elders had prepared a couple of pages of answers to common gospel questions for me to take home, and using them I was able to help Sue understand better why I had joined the Church.

My girlfriend was a more difficult problem. She was a strong Catholic and neither of us knew exactly what to make of the new situation. I had been dating her for two years, but I went off one summer to play baseball and came home a changed person — with a conviction she had never known me to have.

I made a lot of mistakes early after I joined the Church. I knew some answers and I knew the gospel could change people's lives. But I didn't know that not everybody was going to accept those truths immediately. I was so excited I guess I turned some people off.

I had a number of long talks with my girlfriend and her mother, who were fine people. Once they asked me if I wanted to marry a member of the Church. My girlfriend wasn't interested in converting, but I told them, yes, I did want to marry a member. That put a damper on our relationship.

Nearly every time we got together we argued about Joseph Smith or the Book of Mormon, or if Mormons would be the only ones saved. I was just so young in the Church, I kind of blew people away. I was nineteen years old, naive, and a new convert. It took me some time to get used to the fact that I couldn't convert everyone right then and there. I wasn't telling people things in any particular order, either; I would just open up and tell them everything I knew.

One thing I was certain of: I wanted to get married in the temple so I could be with my wife and family for eternity. That made things difficult with my girlfriend, but I couldn't deny my testimony.

Finally I went to my bishop in Portland and talked to him about it. I'll always be grateful for his understanding and advice. It was his advice to break up with her. It wasn't that she was a bad person, but she wasn't a member of the Church and, as a result, I couldn't have married her in the temple.

I don't think everyone knew how important these things were to me. I had left Portland as a certain type of guy, and came back saying I wouldn't marry anyone outside a Mormon temple. No wonder they didn't know what I was talking about. I was committed, but I shouldn't have expected people to grasp that right off. I expected everyone to understand and it didn't work out. We ended by breaking up.

At first I couldn't understand why my whole family didn't want to immediately join the Church. It took me time to gain patience.

A few years ago I sent Susan and her husband a fifty-gallon drum for Christmas. It was to store water. They didn't know what to think. At first they thought it was a little silly and laughed, but later they told me they were touched that I cared enough to send them something like that. Of course, another reason why it probably didn't go over too well was that I accidentally sent it without paying the shipping charges. Receiving a mysterious fifty-gallon drum and then having to pay charges for it is enough to make anyone wonder.

I was a member of the true church. There were obstacles, but they couldn't change my mind. I had a testimony. The gospel had changed my life, given me direction, and soon would lead me to finding my wife, Nancy.

7 Mission Field or Ball Field?

Shortly after my baptism I began reading the *Church News* and the *Ensign*, noting how often President Spencer W. Kimball requested that every worthy young man serve a mission. I started feeling that it was something I should seriously consider. The prophet's counsel seemed right and clear, and the matter began to be on my mind almost constantly. I would sit up late at night, reading Church literature and thinking of leaving baseball and answering the call.

During the summer of 1976 when I was playing in Savannah, a lady asked me at church one Sunday if I was a missionary. When I told her no, she replied, "Of course you are. We're all missionaries."

The Elders who had taught me the gospel had impressed me greatly, and I had always felt that they were making a special commitment, spending two years to teach people their message.

I finally decided I would get through the season and try to make a decision before the next spring.

That fall I was called up for my first trip to the major leagues, and after the season ended I began hearing talk that I might be catching in Atlanta the next year. All the while I was having these thoughts about giving up baseball.

I didn't go to instructional league after the season, because I wanted to sort things out and decide what to do. My parents had moved to Pittsburgh, and I went there to visit and talk over my thoughts with them. It was an emotional time because I knew I wanted to play baseball, but more than that I wanted to do what the Lord required. Along with questions about serving a mission, I also wanted to go to the temple, but understood that usually people my age didn't go there until they were ready to leave on a mission or get married.

I told Mom and Dad I was thinking of quitting baseball and explained how much the Church meant to me. I knew they wanted me to play baseball and that they, too, had an investment in my career. But once again their support was there. They told me they wanted me to do what I felt was right and they would back either decision.

When Dad put his arm around my shoulders and said they would support me in my choice, it took a great load off my mind. Kids always seem to want their parents' approval, but I was attending a church they didn't and was now thinking of completely changing my life's direction. I hadn't been sure how they would react.

I went to Portland to spend the winter and make a decision. I began talking to my bishop and the Beaverton Stake president. We talked about the things I wanted to accomplish in baseball and in the Church.

During one visit with the stake president, Harold Heaton, he asked me if I had heard of Elder Paul H. Dunn. I knew he was a General Authority, but that was about all.

President Heaton told me Elder Dunn had been a professional baseball player and perhaps he could give me some advice. Since becoming a stake president he had gotten to know Elder Dunn, so he placed a call to Salt Lake City and got Elder Dunn on the line. President Heaton said he had a ballplayer in his office who had some questions. An interview was set up, and I began making plans to drive to Salt Lake City for the visit.

When I arrived the next week I was apprehensive, but Elder Dunn was understanding and gracious. He told me of a few of his baseball experiences. When the conversation turned more serious, he told me that in some cases one could go to the temple without going on a mission or being married.

We talked about my desire to do what the Lord wanted, and I said I would drop baseball then and there if it was the thing I should do. I had been praying diligently about the matter but as yet hadn't been able to find the answer.

Elder Dunn counseled with me about the benefits of both choices. He really helped me see things better, then left the decision to me and told me I should continue seeking the Lord's help.

About this time the Braves' owner, Ted Turner, was wondering what was going on. I had never negotiated on a contract; I just customarily signed and sent it back. But I held off that winter, not wanting to commit myself to baseball until I was sure of my plans.

Ted was nervous, which is understandable. He didn't know a whole lot about the Mormons and all of a sudden he started hearing that his No. 1 draft choice was thinking of quitting baseball and maybe leaving the country to preach.

He made some phone calls, including some to me, wanting to know who was "in charge of the Church" in Atlanta. He was referred to the mission president, Russell Taylor, who presided over the Atlanta area. Ted asked him if I could serve a mission in Atlanta while I was playing ball.

Ted also went on record as having facetiously said that if I left on a mission he would kill himself, his family, and his grandmother; but if I stayed, they'd all become Mormons. Neither took place.

President Taylor was another great influence on me. He was very understanding and supportive, telling me that a mission would be a great blessing but that I could also spread the gospel as a baseball player.

I kept trying to get off by myself to sort things out in my prayers and make sure my decision was the right one.

I took great stock in the counsel of the leaders I spoke with. None pushed me towards my decision. My patriarchal blessing said it was not known then whether I should go on a full-time mission, but if I did I should accept it with full dedication. It also said I would be able to serve in missionary opportunities with my associates.

My brief stay with the Braves at the end of the 1976 season and my chances to start for them in 1977 never really entered the picture. I only wanted to do the Lord's will, to make a decision and feel right.

Finally, during the winter, I felt my prayers were answered. I had decided I should wait on a full-time mission and represent the Church in my work. I felt assured that the Lord knew my desires and concerns and that he would prepare a way for me to accomplish his will. And it has been a blessing, because I have since had the opportunity to speak of my beliefs to many people in many places, for which I am grateful.

Often I am asked by young athletes in the Church what they should do about a mission. I would never encourage someone faced with that decision to put their sports above their responsibility to serve the Lord. I did not serve a full-time mission, and I must account for my decisions someday, as will all of us. In my case the timing and circumstances and the counsel I received all played a part in the decision. Young people faced with that choice, however, cannot rightfully use me as an excuse for their not serving a mission. Too, they should remember that the odds aren't very good on playing professional sports as a career.

BYU athletes have shown that you can serve a mission and still follow a career in sports afterward. Some BYU football players have done so, and Devin Durrant made it to the National Basketball Association after serving a mission. There is no reason to concern yourself that a mission will hurt your chances in sports.

BYU football coach LaVell Edwards has said that when you go on a mission you usually return with a better understanding of what you want and your priorities are lined-up better. An athlete will usually have better work habits and a clearer idea of why he is in athletics.

The opportunity to play sports will wait, but sometimes a mission won't.

Few of the young people who ask me what they should do are going to be a No. 1 draft choice. The Braves had invested some $50,000 in my signing bonus and three years of training in the minor leagues to ensure that I would one day play for them. My chances were better from the start than most players'. Just wanting to be a professional athlete or being a good high school or college athlete shouldn't be the reason for skipping a mission.

My advice is to be certain you do what the Lord wants, not what you want. I made my decision after I was sure that I could do the Lord's will and accept either decision without question.

One of my greatest goals is to serve a fulltime mission. I yearn for that opportunity. It's always in the back of my mind. It's an experience one can gain in no other way. So as Nancy and I make our plans for the future, a mission is always included.

As for Ted Turner's concerns that I was going on a mission, he may not have realized it, but my mission would be served for the time being there, playing baseball for the Atlanta Braves.

Part II

Career

8 Throwing It Away

Spring training in 1977 didn't arrive a moment too soon. I was raring to go.

Everything was falling into place for me. I felt at peace with myself over the decision to stay with baseball, and knew the Lord would give me opportunities to do missionary work there. I had gotten my first taste of the major leagues in 1976; and while playing at that level was a little scary at first, I ended the year confident I could make it in the "bigs." And finally, during the off-season the Braves had handed me the starting catcher's job. I couldn't believe it. The job was mine to lose, they told me.

Well, to make a long story short, I did lose it — and lost it in a very embarrassing way. In a matter of a few months I went from being on top of the world to almost losing my career.

Though it's still a little painful to think back on that part of my life, I learned some valuable lessons, and now I guess I can say I'm thankful I had to overcome that adversity. It helped make me grateful for everything the Lord has blessed me with since then. And I learned to not take anything for granted — even something simple like throwing a baseball.

Throwing is one of the elementary baseball skills—like running, hitting, and catching. There aren't many jobs in the game for players who can't throw well. To be honest, my throwing arm is what earned me that potential starting position with Atlanta. My hitting was okay, but it was nothing special, and the coaches were willing to work with me on that part of my game. But I'm sure my arm is what caught the scouts' attention back in Portland, got me drafted, and kept me moving up through the minors. When writers compared me with Johnny Bench, they were talking about my throwing, not my batting.

Imagine, then, waking up one morning and suddenly discovering you can't throw accurately, after years and years of doing it so much it becomes almost as natural as breathing. That's what happened to me, almost overnight, it seemed. It was pretty frightening, considering that my arm was what got me there in the first place. My throws to second base, throws to third base, even throws back to the pitcher became an adventure. I use this analogy a lot, and maybe it's overdramatic, but it's like an artist waking up one morning and discovering he can't draw even a simple flower. Or a great pianist finding he can't get through "Chopsticks."

When I look back, I can't put my finger on the source of my throwing problem. I had never had pinpoint accuracy with my throws. In fact, I remember my parents telling me that one fellow, when he found out I would be catching that day, said something like, "Oh no. Murphy will either hit it out of the park or throw it out of the park."

My throwing wasn't *that* bad. Sure, I threw my share away, but that's part of the game. You slip while setting to throw, you don't get a good grip on the ball, the batter distracts you, or you just plain uncork a wild one. It had never been a big problem. I'd make a bad throw, figure out why, and correct it the next time.

If I had to pinpoint the beginning of my throwing problem, it would probably be an incident at Richmond, Virginia, late in the 1976 season. I had been with the Double-A team at Savannah, Georgia, all season, but was called up to the Triple-A team after Richmond made it to the playoffs.

I was catching the final game of the championship series. It was the last inning with one out and the bases loaded. Jack McKeon (later famous as "Trader Jack," the general manager of the San Diego Padres), our manager, had a conference with us on the pitcher's mound. Rick Camp, who had a good sinkerball, was pitching. "Don't worry about it," Jack said. "Just throw your sinker in there and you'll get a ground ball. Throw it to Murph and he'll throw it to first. We'll get a double play."

That's *almost* what happened. Camp threw a good pitch, and the batter hit it right back to him. He threw it to me for the first out. I threw it into right field. We lost the game and the series.

I didn't think about my mistake too much then, because, as I mentioned earlier, I was called up to the major leagues—ironically, right after blowing that game.

My arm was somewhat erratic in the three weeks I spent with Atlanta at the end of the season, but I passed it off as nervousness—it *was* my first trip to the big leagues.

After making my mission decision following the 1976 season, I started working out regularly at Portland State, near my home. I had thought a lot about the balls I'd thrown away near the end of the season, and I was determined to work my way out of it. But the more I thought and fretted about it, the worse it seemed to get. I was really forcing my throws and still having big problems with accuracy. I studied the mechanics of my motion over and over, but couldn't find anything wrong. The throws just weren't getting there consistently. Now I realize that I was letting my mind interfere with what should have come naturally. I'll tell you, though, I sure couldn't figure it out back then.

But things were going so well in every other way. I headed to Florida early in 1977 with every confidence that I'd get my throwing problem taken care of. Spring training is good for working out the little bugs in your game.

Those first few weeks of workouts were certainly exciting. Everyone was talking to me and treating me like I was going to make the big-league club. And the attention from the media was flattering. It seems that almost every day I'd open the paper and see a story comparing me with such-and-such big league player or predicting that I would be the Braves' catcher for many years to come. Pretty heady stuff for a twenty-year-old kid!

I still hadn't proven anything on the field yet, though things weren't going too badly. I was throwing well in workouts and felt sure the problem was gone. I was working hard to repay the trust the Braves had in me and trying to live up to all those nice things I read in the papers.

Several people said later on that I may have put too much pressure on myself because of the team's and media's high expectations of me, and that's how my throwing problem started again — all that pressure. I tried to be too good, they said, and wouldn't relax and let it all fall into place.

I don't know about that, because I had always handled pressure well before. I do admit I felt some anxiety because I was expected to make the team. All I know is that when the exhibition games started, I began to throw poorly again.

It was strange. During warmups I would usually whip the ball around the infield with no problem. The few times I would throw one away, it wasn't a big deal to the others, but it was to me. The "problem" was starting to plant itself in the back of my mind again.

During games, even exhibition games, there is no place for errors. In exhibitions they try to simulate real-game conditions to see how the players will react. When it came to throwing out runners, unfortunately, quite often I didn't do it very well. I did get my share out. But when I threw to second base, I had no idea where the ball would go.

As you can imagine, the word got around. It seemed that everyone was trying to steal bases off me. In fact, I'll bet they would have taken off for home plate if I had had to throw the ball there. Throws were bouncing just in back of the pitcher's mound and flying ten feet over the second baseman's head. There was nothing wrong with my velocity — in fact, I threw out a handful of runners with really bad throws that sometimes required spectacular catches by the second basemen and short-stops. It's hard to describe how embarrassing this all was. I mean, these were the major leagues, where players have overcome problems like this. I was supposed to be the Braves' catcher for the next fifteen years, and I couldn't even throw the ball to second base.

One day we went to Fort Lauderdale to play the New York Yankees in an exhibition game. While we were warming up, I heard one of our coaches tell Billy Martin, then manager of the Yankees, "Hey, watch this kid throw. He's got an unbelievable arm." Well, I wanted to impress him, so I put a little something extra on my next throw. It bounced ten feet in front of the base. The one after that went way over the player's head. I could not make a good throw to any base. Quite an exhibition for the manager of the New York Yankees! "Well," I thought, "that's one team I won't get traded to."

Mr. Martin is a smart man, and you can guess what happened the moment one of his players reached first base. He was off for second, and my throw was off to center field. Another Yankee tried to steal third base and I threw it into left field. I got so flustered that I couldn't even throw it back to the pitcher. I'd either dribble it to him or make him leap to catch it. I started walking almost halfway to the mound and underhanding it to him like a softball. Finally, Dave Bristol, our manager, ended this humiliating exhibition by taking me out in the *middle* of an inning. Sure, getting removed that way was embarrassing, but no more embarrassing than what I was doing on the field.

They sent me to a nearby practice field to work with Chris Cannizzaro, a former major-league catcher, and two other coaches. They gave me a target to throw at, and I couldn't hit the thing. I've never been so frustrated in my life. The coaches were all examining the mechanics of my throwing, but I knew the problem wasn't there. It was in my head.

That night I returned to my room and cried. I couldn't understand what was happening to me. Here I was being handed my big chance, the one I'd always dreamed of, practically on a silver platter. And I was blowing it. I don't ever remember feeling lower in my life.

It was more of the same the next few weeks. I'd uncork a perfect throw and beat a fast runner by a mile, then toss the next two into center field. I just couldn't control it. Soon, it was getting to where the Braves could hardly play me in a game. I wasn't hitting all that well, either, and another catcher, Biff Pocoroba, was hitting above .400 and throwing the ball where he was supposed to. I could see my opportunity steadily slipping away, and the harder I tried to save it, the worse it seemed to get. I'd wake up each morning and immediately start getting nervous about going to the ballpark. I'd wonder how much I'd have to throw that day, which is silly because a catcher always has to throw. Baseball wasn't fun any more.

My poor dad sat through some of these painful games in Florida. He tried to make me feel better. "Son," he told me one day, "if they were stealing center field, they wouldn't have a chance." And Barry Bonnell tried to cheer me up by telling me what a great play we were perfecting—I throw the ball into center field, then he throws the runner out at third base. I laugh at these now, but nothing seemed very funny to me then.

Finally, on one of the first cuts, the Braves sent me across the row of bushes that divided the major- and minor-league complexes. (I'd always thought how appropriate it was to have this as the border between the major and "bush" leagues.) I was in the minors again. I knew it was coming—the Braves had no choice. I was relieved, and the pressure seemed to disappear. But I was also mad at myself for blowing what could have been a once-in-a-lifetime chance, and for letting a lot of people down in the process.

I'm sometimes asked why I feel such loyalty to the Braves. I think it stems as much from the way they treated me during hard times as what they've done for me in recent years. Other teams might have given up on me, but the Braves' management, from Ted Turner on down, went out of their way to offer encouragement and support. They could have ended my career but instead made gestures like sending Hank Aaron on a special trip to Florida to talk to me. One man who especially went out of his way to help me was Bill Lucas. Bill was director of minor league personnel—in other words, my boss. But he was much more than a boss. He was a close friend and one of my biggest supporters. We had a unique relationship, and it was one of the saddest days of my life when he suddenly passed away in 1979.

The Braves' management knew how upset I was about my throwing problem and handled it in just the right way. Rather than just shipping me off to the minors without a word, they pointed out in detail why it was being done (though I knew). They encouraged me to solve my problem as soon as possible, promising me a plane flight south from Richmond as soon as I did.

The problem, and the answer, were both within me. I just had to find out where.

That, I would soon find out, was not as easy as I thought it would be. Even though the pressure was off while playing in Richmond, my throwing all through 1977 was erratic. Now I even joke about inventing a new statistic. You've heard about the "hit by pitcher" (HBP) category? I started HBC—"hit by catcher." I nailed my first pitcher on opening night. Poor Al

Autry. He delivered a pitch to the plate as a runner took off for second base. He then crouched down as low as he could, as he was supposed to. But my throw to second skipped off the front part of the pitcher's mound and hit him in the back. I don't know if the look on his face showed more shock or amusement. I ran out to apologize to him and he said something like, "That's okay, Sarge, let's just get this next one out." If I'd hurt Al, or if he'd gotten mad at me, it would have been pretty devastating. I might have been tempted to throw in the towel right there.

It was still so puzzling. Some throws were right on the money, but others were as wild as they could be. The center fielder would start sprinting in the moment he saw an attempted steal, half expecting the ball to come to him. And infielders got plenty of practice taking my throws on one hop and still making a diving tag. I threw out more runners than I care to admit with tosses like that. Tommie Aaron, my manager at Richmond, once joked that I threw out more runners with bad throws than any other catcher in the league did with good ones! Unfortunately, that wasn't a talent that would get me back to the majors.

Luckily, I was also in the middle of one of the best hitting streaks I've ever had, even to this day. I was usually around .250 or .260 my first three years in the minors. That wasn't great, but it was good enough to keep them interested in my defense and my arm. And now that my arm had abandoned me . . .

But at least for the first half of that 1977 season at Richmond, I was batting more than 100 points above my usual level. It was a totally new and fun experience to look in the paper and see my name among the league leaders in home runs, runs batted in, *and* batting average. This three-month streak couldn't have come at a better time in my career. And it's just as big a mystery to me today as my throwing problem. Maybe my defensive shortcomings caused me to bear down more when I was hitting, to tell myself, "You've got to make up for the ball you just threw, or are going to throw, away." I don't know. But I do know I owe what hitting success I've had in the major leagues to the confidence I gained at Richmond that spring.

At least I was helping the team in some way. But my progress at the plate still wasn't greatly affecting my performance behind the plate. So when my bat inevitably cooled down the last few months of the season, the doubts I felt at spring training crept back again. Occasionally, Tommie Aaron was forced to take me out or play me at designated hitter, since Pete Varney, our other catcher, was playing so well. Watching Pete throw with such ease didn't help my mounting frustrations. "Why can't I figure this thing out?" I'd ask myself over and over. In some of these moments I'd actually look for an excuse to quit. "If I hurt my knee again like I did in high school, that's it," I told myself. "That's the end of my career." And, to tell you the truth, I probably would have been relieved if the Braves had released me after that season.

Thank goodness the club had more faith in me than I did. I was called up again after our year had ended in Richmond and got quite a bit of September playing time with Atlanta. My throwing problem didn't get worse or better—it was just there, almost like a permanent part of my life I would just have to get used to. Still, I was back in the majors again and the organization was as supportive as ever. My hitting picked up once more, and I ended the season with the best overall batting average (.306) I'd ever had as a professional.

Among my hits that season were my first two major league home runs—both in the same game at San Diego. Now, anyone who knows me well can tell you I don't have the greatest memory. But I can still recall that first home run vividly. Randy Jones, a tough man to hit home runs off, was pitching. I hit the ball to left field and it cleared the big outfield wall they used to have at Jack Murphy Stadium. All those times I'd fantasized while growing up about hitting a home run in the big leagues— well, it was as thrilling as I thought it would be. The second came off Rollie Fingers, which was lucky, because Rollie was one of the best relief pitchers in the history of the game. I knew I wouldn't hit many more off him (and I didn't). But what a dream game! It was all capped off when Eddie Haas, the first hitting instructor I had had in the minors (and later our manager for a brief stint in 1985—but more on that later), came up and shook my hand, sort of hugged me as he put his arm around me, and congratulated me. It seems like a little thing, but after all my ups and downs, and after four years of playing in the minor leagues, having someone who meant so much to my development there in the dugout was very special.

All in all, then, things looked better as 1977 ended. There

were still questions. My defense wasn't yet major-league caliber. I went to play winter ball in the Dominican Republic and really concentrated on my catching, but my throws were still as accurate as a shotgun blast. I was thinking to myself that I might not be catching much longer, but since my hitting was improving, maybe the Braves could "hide" me at first base. I never did play first down there, but one day Tommie Aaron asked if I'd consider trying it sometime. Hey, I was ready to try anything.

Like Aesop, I tried to find a moral to this story. If I had to sum it up, it might be this: The Lord doesn't judge us on the trials we encounter in life, but on our reaction to those trials.

I was asked to speak at a fireside in Richmond, and the only topic I could think of was adversity. I started reading what people had said about the topic and came across something by James E. Talmage that has stayed in my mind ever since. He said you can either grow or shrink from adversity and it can either sour your disposition and spirit or help you get closer to the Lord. I started thinking a lot about that and told myself no matter what happened, I was going to stay close to the Lord. I realized this was a problem I had brought on myself and I had to work it through. The Lord didn't give it to me. It wasn't a punishment or a sign. I figured I could learn from it or quit from it. And though from my story you can see I didn't always handle it as I should, I know now that I grew from those months, and I'm better today for having passed through that adversity.

Later on, while in the Dominican Republic, I had the chance to read *Jesus the Christ*. What a wonderful book! It only reinforced what I had already read about adversity. How could I complain about my trials after reading what the Savior went through?

I benefited from my time in the Dominican Republic in another way, too. I had a lot of time to think about what is really important in life. Being down there made me appreciate what I'd been blessed with. I still remember sitting in the locker room in Florida the day I was sent down to the minors. Paul Snyder, a minor-league official for the Braves, saw I was down in the dumps. He came up to me and said, "Don't worry too much about this. Just be grateful you still have your health." Mr.

Snyder had suffered a stroke and had returned to work only after having learned to write and read all over again.

Know what? He was right. So I did have a throwing problem. So what? I had my health and an awful lot more. I had a great family and the true gospel of Jesus Christ.

And, thanks to the Braves, it looked like I'd have another year to prove myself.

9 Dimes into Diamonds

Okay, I admit it. I went to BYU after the 1978 season hoping to find a wife.

But there were other reasons, too. Because I'd signed with the Braves right out of high school instead of going to Arizona State, I'd missed out on the college experience. I wanted to fill this empty spot in my life—there were a lot of things I knew I had to learn.

And since my baptism, I'd never lived in a place where the Church was a big part of the everyday environment. I thought that would be nice, even if only for a few months. I also knew there were a lot of things I had yet to learn about the gospel.

As you might suspect, there aren't many chances for a baseball-playing LDS bachelor to meet the right sort of people to associate with socially. In the baseball world it's much, much easier to fall in with the wrong crowd than to keep high standards. I didn't socialize much because of this.

BYU seemed like the best place to help me meet these needs in my life. I recall my first visit to the campus in 1976, while visiting Ernie Thompson, my LDS friend from high school. The place was beautiful. And I couldn't believe how everyone would stop walking and stand still when the national anthem was played each morning. I remember thinking what a neat place it was and how I'd like to go to school there during the off-season — that is, if they'd accept me. I wasn't always the best student in high school.

I'd just finished my first full season in the major leagues in 1978, and the Braves made me feel secure about my future with them. So I decided this was as good a time as any to take a break from baseball and try a little college life. BYU did accept me, and I spent some of the happiest months of my life in Provo.

I had a blast going to classes and studying again. The religion courses, the devotionals, the family home evening groups, the involvement in a student ward — the whole atmosphere was great. I even had the privilege of being the home-teaching companion of James Arrington, who did the one-man "Here's Brother Brigham" stage show. I felt honored and learned a lot from his wisdom and knowledge.

And yes, I did meet my wife at BYU. Nobody believes me when I tell them this, but she was the first girl I met there. She really was! But the story gets pretty complicated from there.

I arrived at Provo in the middle of the semester. The athletic department was kind enough to find me a place to live, but I was still uncomfortable because I didn't know any of my room-mates. I was pretty nervous, then, when I walked up to the apartment door and knocked. A girl answered. That made me even more nervous. Here she was, standing there in one of those famous BYU gym suits. I found out later she was a cheerleader named Nancy Thomas and had just finished practice. I thought I might be in the wrong place, but I stammered something like, "I think I'm supposed to be moving in." She went back to get the guys, and they welcomed me and helped me move in. What an initiation to BYU!

Nancy was there visiting her boyfriend and my future room-mate. They had been going together for quite a while. In fact, I learned she had even waited for him while he went on a mission.

I settled in and gradually got used to my new surroundings. I dated some, but mostly went out with groups of friends. I tried to be diligent in my schoolwork and worked out often to keep in shape. I was having a lot of fun.

And Nancy? Sure, I was impressed by her. I recall telling another roommate I would like to marry a girl like her someday.

She loved people and loved the gospel. She always made me feel comfortable and was easy to talk to. But it would have to be someone *like* Nancy, because she was my roommate's girlfriend. We did become friends—in the unique sort of way a boyfriend's roommates do.

I left Provo for spring training in February 1979 with many great memories and lots of new friends—and Nancy was one of the best of them. Our birthdays fall on the same day in March, so we got in touch to wish each other a happy birthday. She was fine, enjoying school. I was fine, enjoying spring training.

The 1979 season began, and I wasn't able to think much about BYU anymore. But what a year it was starting out to be! I was off to the best start in my career. I was playing every day and really beginning to feel comfortable with my game. Then, one day in May, I lunged to the right to catch one of Phil Niekro's fluttering knuckleballs. The next morning I could hardly walk—I'd torn the cartilage in my knee, and it would have to be operated on. I would be sidelined for nearly two months, a prospect I found pretty depressing. Thank goodness Barry Bonnell was on the team with me. I think Barry's favorite pastime, next to getting me married off, was to keep my spirits up. (Come to think of it, maybe he knew the two went hand-in-hand.)

During the late stages of my recovery, I'd go to the club-house daily for therapy. I was in the training room one day late in June when one of my teammates, Joe Nolan, walked in and said, "Murph, you have a message here from a Nancy Thomas. We didn't know you were here, so we just took a message." I still vividly remember what happened when he told me that. The most special feeling came over me. I couldn't explain it. And I had no idea why she was calling—maybe she'd heard I'd been injured and wanted to tell me my friends back in Provo were thinking of me. I don't know. All I know is that I had the neatest feeling inside of me, and I was excited about it.

I tried calling Nancy, but she wasn't home. We finally connected the next day. She had heard about my injury and wanted to make sure I wasn't down. She told me things weren't going too well for her, either. She and her boyfriend had broken up. I was sorry to hear that. I really was. I knew how close they were and how hard it must have been on both of them. I didn't want to see either of them unhappy. Well, we tried to cheer each other up the best we could, and I think it worked. The more we

talked, the more we discovered how much we enjoyed talking to
each other. We called just about daily for the next several days,
and the conversations seemed to get longer and more serious. I
was beginning to understand the feeling I'd had in the training
room.

Something special was happening, but I still didn't feel right
about becoming anything more than a good friend to Nancy. I
called my sister, Susan, at work one day to ask her advice.
Susan had met Nancy during a visit to BYU. I explained the
situation and how Nancy had recently broken off her engage-
ment. Would it be okay to keep calling her or was it still too
soon? Susan is very wise, and her counsel helped me put things
in perspective. Basically, she told me if I felt good about it to go
ahead.

It did feel good to me, so we continued running up a rather
substantial phone bill. That's when my other "coach," Barry,
stepped in: "Murph, you've got to get her out here. Let's go get a
plane ticket and send it to her." That sounded like a good idea,
so we flew Nancy into Atlanta, and she stayed with Barry and
his wife, Stefnie. Our relationship continued to blossom through
the summer, just as I suspected it would from that first feeling
in the training room. She came to Atlanta a few times, or flew to
the West Coast with her folks when we played there. The rest of
our communicating took place by phone, and we still have the
bills to prove it — $80 for one call from Cincinnati, about $800
for one month's bill.

It was an odd courtship, but we still managed to have plenty
of good experiences together. The first time I took her to one of
our ballgames, as we were driving up to the stadium she said,
"Wait a minute; is this like Willie Mays?" She had seen Willie
Mays play when she lived in the San Francisco area, but that
was about the extent of her baseball knowledge. My roommates
at BYU liked to kid her about that and told her one day, "Nancy,
do you know what Dale does? He plays professional baseball."
"Oh," she responded, "does he play with Willie Mays?" Willie
had long since retired from the game.

Even if she didn't know baseball, she knew me and how to
make me happy. Nancy has a great sense of humor, and she can
really put me in my place sometimes. But she also knows *when*
to use it. Once, the Braves held a Mormon Night at the stadium,
and members from all over the Southeast came to see the game.
Elder Paul Dunn was there, along with many other Church

officials. Nancy had flown into town, too. Boy, did I want to have a big game and impress all those people—especially Nancy. But I didn't. I went 0-for-4 and struck out at least a couple of times. After the game Nancy and I went out to eat—I thought I'd try to impress her with my poise, anyway. I proceeded to get lost in downtown Atlanta, and for quite a while we had no idea where we were. I then pulled out from a curb, and a taxi almost hit us. By this time I was really shook up. Nancy wanted to say something, but she looked over at me and thought the better of it. A few minutes later, after I'd started to relax a little, she said, "Do you know what I was going to say when that cab almost hit you?"

"No, what?"

"Don't worry, that would have been the first thing you hit tonight!" We laughed and laughed. As usual, her consideration, sense of humor—and timing—were faultless.

As I said before, Nancy had everything I could hope for in an eternal companion. I'm sure her upbringing had a lot to do with that. Her parents, Claude and Bonnie Thomas, are some of the greatest people you'd ever want to meet. Nancy was born in Albuquerque, New Mexico, the third of six children. Claude was in the Air Force, then retired to enter medical school at the University of Utah. Nancy lived in Gridley, California, for several years, and then American Fork, Utah, after her father started his medical practice. She went to BYU after graduating from American Fork High School in 1975. Her folks now live in Richfield, Utah, where he has a family practice. They're great in-laws. And they were awfully patient with some outrageous phone bills while we were getting to know each other!

With all the talking Nancy and I did, there were some things that didn't have to be mentioned. Like marriage, for instance. Our relationship grew so easily and naturally that marriage was a foregone conclusion. It was more a matter of when and where. I am, by nature, a very methodical and deliberate person. I don't like to make snap decisions. But even with the little bit of foot-dragging I did to mull the whole thing over, it was only two months after our first telephone call that I officially "popped the question."

She was expecting it, but wasn't quite sure where it would come—or how. I decided to propose in San Francisco, the most beautiful city in my National League travels. One problem: We would be leaving for our West Coast road trip in a few days, and

I didn't have the ring, nor the faintest idea how to go about getting one. My sister, Susan, once more came to the rescue. She worked for a jeweler and agreed to pick out just the right diamond and setting. The day we were to leave, she bought the ring a seat on an airplane and shipped it from Portland to Atlanta. I was sure nervous while waiting for it, and sure excited when it arrived, and sure late to meet the team for the trip (which, as many people know, is nothing new).

I proposed to Nancy at a park near the Golden Gate Bridge, which was pretty romantic. Luckily, she said yes, so I decided to give her the ring that night. We had dinner at a nice restaurant. One of my hobbies was magic, and I was forever turning dimes into quarters out of a napkin for Nancy. I told her, "Let me show you this magic trick." She said, "Dale, I've already seen it; you've shown it to me a million times." "You haven't seen this one," I said. I turned the dime into the ring, instead of a quarter. Not quite as romantic as Golden Gate Park, but lots of fun.

I'm not one to make a scene in public, but I found myself walking up to total strangers on the street and telling them, "We just got engaged!" They say love makes you do crazy things.

I may have been a little crazy, but I knew I was doing the right thing. My patriarchal blessing told me that when I found the right girl, I would have no question about it. One day before I met Nancy I was in the Los Angeles Temple. I ran into Elder Hartman Rector, Jr., whom I had met at a Mormon Night game in San Diego while he was a mission president there. We talked for a few minutes, then he asked me if I was married. When I told him no, he gave me some great advice. He told me to make sure I obtained spiritual confirmation about the girl I wanted to marry, just as I had with my testimony of the gospel.

I remembered the feeling I had when I prayed about the truthfulness of the Book of Mormon. And I later realized the feeling I had in the training room *was* quite similar. It was a very strong feeling, like a burning within me. As I got to know Nancy better, it kept getting stronger and stronger, telling me that she was definitely the "right one."

Well, who was I to argue with that? We were married on October 29, 1979, in the Salt Lake Temple, a little over a year after we first met and about four months after we began our long distance relationship. The Bonnells were there with us. Elder Dunn was nice enough to perform the ceremony. When we walked into the sealing room at the temple, he looked around, then at me and said, "This is the biggest on-deck circle you've ever been in." It sure was. It was the happiest one, too.

A few days later we were shopping in Provo. The sales clerk found out we were newlyweds and she told us, "Just stick it out. The first couple of weeks are horrible, but believe me, marriage gets a lot better." Nancy and I looked at each other and said, "Wow, if this is going to get better, it will be great!"

It is great — and still getting better.

10 Finding a Niche

When I think back to my early years in the major leagues, I honestly wonder how I could still have a job there. It's funny how things manage to work out sometimes. A lot of things had to fall into place for me, for which I'm grateful.

After my brief trips to the majors at the end of the 1976 and 1977 seasons, I finally made the big team in 1978. It was a thrill, but I was realistic about my status. My throwing arm, which I felt had really brought me this far, was still inconsistent and not yet major-league caliber. But my hitting, which had always been "just good enough," had improved dramatically.

So now my bat was keeping me in the major leagues. And I realized there were plenty of players around who could hit *and* play defense. I was in a race against time to straighten out my throwing problem before the Braves would find one of these players. It's not that the club was impatient with me—far from it. I don't know of another organization that would have given me as many chances. It's just that Atlanta, like any other team, has to find players who can help win ballgames for them. If I couldn't do it, someone else would.

Even though I was excited, I was far from feeling secure. I was asked to move to first base, since my throwing was still not up to par. Learning a whole new position didn't excite me too much, but I thought I'd have a better chance to make the team there than at catcher. I think they were hiding me at first base until my throwing problem was taken care of—then I'd move back to catcher.

A position switch is always traumatic. It's like a football player moving from running back to defensive back. There's a whole new set of skills to master. But it sure beat unemployment, so I worked hard to try to make myself into a good first baseman. The results speak for themselves, I'm afraid to report. I led the league in errors at the position, some feat considering I also played about twenty games at catcher. My performance behind the plate was improving, but not enough for them to take me away from first, despite my errors there.

I didn't exactly tear up the place with my bat, either. But I did provide fans with plenty of relief from summer heat with the wind from my bat missing the ball. You guessed it. I also led the league in strikeouts with 145, or about one out of every four times I stepped up to the plate.

It was an eye-opening initiation to the *real* world of the major leagues. Going up for 162 games is a lot different from going up for three weeks. Adrenalin can carry a player for three weeks, but skill eventually prevails over six months. I must admit, I wasn't totally prepared for this level of competition day-in and day-out. And I had to learn to concentrate and pace myself better for the entire season. It's called enduring to the end, I guess. My batting average suffered as I learned these lessons, and I finished the season around .225. No, that's not very good.

My first full major-league season wasn't all disappointment, though. Sometime during 1977 at Richmond I gained confidence that I could hit for power more consistently. I had started a weight training program and began to see balls that a year earlier would have been long outs suddenly carry a few extra feet and clear the fence. Luckily, that confidence carried over into the 1978 season at Atlanta. Though my batting average and strikeouts weren't impressive, I guess I hit enough home runs and drove in enough runs to keep the Braves interested in me for another year.

Four of those RBI came in what I still consider the most memorable game of my career. My parents were living in Pittsburgh, but were about to be transferred to England. We usually make two trips each season to Pittsburgh, and one of them happened to come just before they were to move. On the last night of the series, Dad and Mom's friends threw a going-away party for them at Three Rivers Stadium. I wanted to do well, anyway, since this would be the last game my parents would see for a while. Having so many of their friends at the stadium made me doubly determined. (That doesn't guarantee anything, though. Remember how I played at Mormon Night in Atlanta, when I wanted to impress Nancy!)

We were down by three runs late in the game and had the bases loaded when I came to bat. Kent Tekulve, one of the toughest relievers in the league, was pitching. He throws a "submarine-type" sinking pitch that's nearly impossible to hit in the air. He handled me pretty easily on the first two pitches, running the count to no balls, two strikes. Then, for some reason, he threw me an overhand curve ball. I knew I wouldn't see one of those again from him, so I swung as hard as I could. The ball really carried and went over the fence. As I ran around the bases, somewhat dazed, I don't know who was more shocked—Tekulve or me. It was my first career grand slam and it ended up winning the game, normally great thrills, but it meant so much more to be able to do it under those circumstances for my parents and their friends. Afterwards, I walked around the stadium, looking for Dad. Needless to say, when we found each other we had plenty of excitement—and tears—to share. I'll remember that night as long as I live.

I felt I'd learned a lot in my rookie season and was anxious to show it in 1979. Though I had gone to BYU in the off-season, I'd still worked hard to get ready for my second year.

Everything was now going my way. Even though my defense was still shaky, other aspects of my game were really clicking. By late May I was among the league leaders in batting average, home runs, and runs batted in. I'd just compiled one of the longest hitting streaks of my career and had hit three home runs in a game for the first time. I was being played semi-regularly at catcher, which I enjoyed much more than first base. My confidence level was at an all-time high.

But things can change so quickly in life. It was then that I injured my knee catching Phil Niekro's knuckleball. This wasn't a big surprise. I had felt a little popping and clicking in the knee at spring training. When I asked the doctor about it, he told me I'd eventually tear the cartilage and there was no way I could get around it.

But why now? I wondered. Here I was finally proving I belonged in the major leagues. I was on my way to a good season. And now this. I'll admit I was pretty depressed about the course of events, and I searched long and hard for the reason or meaning behind it all.

There's no more helpless feeling than going down with an injury and watching your teammates from the sidelines. One thing about a baseball organization, it always has a replacement ready to step in for you. Very few players are indispensable, and I certainly wasn't at this point in my career. They say some of the best-read pages in *The Sporting News* are the minor-league batting averages. You want to see how the young prospects behind you are doing. It's inevitable—unless you retire at the top of your game, one of these up-and-coming players will eventually earn your job.

My fears may have been exaggerated, but when you're injured you have plenty of time to think about these things and feel sorry for yourself. Again the analogy with an artist: I felt like a painter who knew he was working on the best picture of his life, only to see something destroy it before it could be finished. Would I ever be able to recapture what I had?

Once again, things worked out. I still felt like I was "renting" at first base and just waiting to raise the down payment to "buy" back a permanent spot behind the plate. But at least I had *a* position to return to. I never did hit that season the way I did before I was injured.

But I had a knee that was better than new, and a secure spot on the team for another season (as secure as a fellow without a true position could be). And I often wonder if Nancy and I would have gotten together by telephone if I had not been injured. All in all, 1979 wasn't a bad bargain—lose a little cartilage and gain an eternal companion!

Nancy and I had only a few months of married life behind us when my career took another unusual twist. We were attending BYU again during the off-season when I got a call from Bobby Cox, my manager. He asked if I thought I could play the outfield. I told him I'd be glad to give it a try.

I knew the Braves had recently traded Barry Bonnell, among others, to the Toronto Blue Jays for Chris Chambliss, a power hitter and fine first baseman. I knew it would affect my role on the team, but I wasn't exactly sure how. Maybe they'd try me again at catcher or put me on the bench. Bobby's call cleared everything up and provided a welcome challenge. I was excited about it, so excited that I began practicing catching fly balls the same day. I'd never felt comfortable at first base, and my catching didn't make the team feel comfortable. I knew a little about the outfield and thought to myself, "Well, now I don't have to put so much pressure on myself on defense." The outfield doesn't receive as many plays, and the margin for error, particularly on throws, is a little greater.

That doesn't mean, though, that it's a piece of cake. Nancy and I went to spring training, and I worked and worked and worked at the new position. I was nervous for the first few practices, but then found the increased distance helped my throwing; I began to relax and feel at home there. I played left field in our opening exhibition game, and one of the first batters hit a line-drive base hit down the line. I ran over and backhanded it, then threw it as hard as I could to second. It bounced once, then went right to the base. I thought to myself, "If I had been a catcher, I'd have been in trouble with that throw. But while it wasn't pretty, it got the job done." I found I could relax and just throw from the outfield, and my accuracy improved.

I still felt a little uneasy about the switch as the regular season approached. I knew I would be expected to be a big-league-level outfielder. And, once again, there was a whole new set of skills to learn. Some things, though, would only come with experience. Where do you throw it? When do you try throwing a runner out? When do you dive for a ball? How do you judge where a ball will be hit by the way the pitcher is throwing? The outfield has its own little peculiarities, and each of its three positions is unique. I started in left field, but played plenty of center and right before settling down in center field in 1982, where I've been since.

Once more, I'm grateful the Braves tried so hard to find a spot for me. How they figured that a misfiring catcher and a misfit first baseman could ever make it in the outfield is beyond me. I sometimes joke about the fact that the outfield was the most distant place they could stick me and still keep me in the game. It couldn't have worked out any other way, considering how my defense was going. I still feel I should be catcher, and if I could throw well I would be one right now—I was a good catcher at one time. I wish it would have worked out, because playing that position is a lot of fun.

I know I'm still in baseball today because Ted Turner and Bobby Cox and maybe some other people I don't even know about decided to try me in the outfield. It has worked out well and, who knows, maybe even prolonged my career, considering the daily wear and tear on a catcher. Some writers have called Bobby Cox a genius for this decision, and I don't argue that. Position changes that work out are pretty rare in baseball. Maybe he figured if he tried me in enough places, he'd finally find one I could succeed at.

The irony of this whole situation still amazes me. Here I was the catcher some people were calling the next Johnny Bench, and I end up in the position farthest away from the catcher. On top of that, I was just an adequate hitter when I broke into the major leagues, and my bat kept me there until they found a place for me to play.

More irony? Chris Chambliss took my place at first base. Barry Bonnell, who was traded to Toronto for Chris, vacated the outfield spot I eventually settled into. I knew I would miss Barry's friendship and influence in the clubhouse. But then I found out that Luis Gomez, a convert to the Church of about a year, would be coming to our team from Toronto. I gained another fine friend from that trade.

The 1980 season was a memorable one for me. Not only had I found a new home in the field, but a new life at home. It was my first season as a married ballplayer. Let me tell you, those first several road trips were pretty rough. It wasn't easy to leave Nancy, especially since she was expecting our first child. She pretty well got thrown into the baseball life-style without a lot of preparation. But she adjusted well, just as she has with every new situation in our lives. While I was playing and had something to occupy my mind and time, she mostly just stayed at home. But I seemed to be the one having the most problems adjusting. I piled up phone bills not much different from the ones we had while we were still dating.

Here's an example of how hectic that year was: I was in Montreal on July 31 when I got a call. Nancy was in labor and had been taken to the hospital. Montreal is a long way from Atlanta, but I thought I'd try to make it anyway. I was excused from the team, then rushed to the airport, where I tried to find a combination—any combination—that would get me home. After what seemed like an eternity, I got to Atlanta and headed for the hospital. Chad was born fifteen minutes after I arrived there!

The season went quite well. I finally felt good about my defensive contributions to the team. And though I led the league in strikeouts again, I had easily my best hitting year so far. The position change, plus being a new husband and father, helped me to take the game more seriously. The more I studied it, the more I enjoyed it. This was the first season I felt really secure, thought that I might be able to look forward to a long-term career in baseball. And that was gratifying.

To top it off, I was named to the National League All-Star Team. I'm a little hesitant to mention that, because there were a few other fellows on our team who I felt were more deserving. None of our players had been voted to the team by fans, and rules say the manager must choose at least one representative from each team. It easily could have been Chris Chambliss or Bob Horner or Gary Matthews. But I was picked. Though a part of me wanted to take care of a very pregnant wife during the All-Star break (Chad had not yet made his entrance at this point), another part of me was thrilled to be a part of a game that's every baseball-playing boy's dream.

The game was in Los Angeles and was everything I thought it would be. There were banquets and press conferences and special appearences. And it's a real thrill to be in the same locker room with so many of your baseball heroes.

Chuck Tanner was managing the National League team. I'll always be grateful that he gave me a chance to play, even though he sent me in to hit against "Goose" Gossage, one of the hardest throwing and most intimidating pitchers in the game. As I was getting ready to go up and hit, Tommy Lasorda, manager of the Los Angeles Dodgers and a very funny man, said, "Hey Murphy, don't you worry about a thing. Just everyone in Portland, Oregon, will be watching you hit."

I didn't need *that* to make me nervous. Gossage worked me to one ball and two strikes. Then I swung and hit a long fly ball down the left field line that went just foul. Somehow I had the feeling that would be as close as I would come to hitting a home run off the Goose. I was right. He then threw a nasty pitch I could hardly see, and I cued a weak little grounder to the first baseman.

I did get to play the ninth inning in center field. The National League was leading 4-2 with Bruce Sutter, another great relief pitcher, on the mound. The American League got a runner on base and Lance Parrish, the big catcher from the Detroit Tigers, came up. For just a moment I thought what would happen if Parrish hit a home run to tie the game and send it into extra innings. I was so nervous, I wasn't sure my legs would hold up. But, thank goodness, Bruce finished it off.

The All-Star Game is just an exhibition and doesn't count in the standings. But there's a lot of pride riding on it and both teams really want to win. The best way to describe the feeling in the clubhouse or in the dugout is to compare the game to a one-game playoff. It's pretty intense, but a lot of fun as well. The National League has dominated the game so much in recent years that no new group of NL All-Stars wants to be the one to let the streak end. The 13-3 loss to the American League in 1983 was as painful a defeat as I've ever experienced.

But that '83 game had some other great moments that made up for our loss. It was the fiftieth anniversary of the All-Star Game, and many of the great players of past eras were there to play in a special old-timers' game. I grew up idolizing many of them, and to be in the same room as these men just about took my breath away. I was excited when I found out I'd be sharing a locker with Stan Musial, one of the greatest hitters in baseball history. Mr. Musial ended up getting ill and couldn't make it, which really disappointed me. But I did get to see and meet Willie Mays, my number-one hero as a boy, and Johnny Bench, whom I wanted so much to emulate as a catcher. What did I do when I met all these great players? What any other red-blooded baseball fan would have done. I got their autographs.

I've had the privilege of playing in several All-Star Games. I think the greatest honor that can come to a player is to be voted an All-Star by baseball fans, and it humbles me when they choose me. While three days off in the middle of the season would be nice, it doesn't compare with the thrill of rubbing shoulders with the best in your business. I'm always amazed, as I look around, that I'm there with them and that they respect me as much as I do them. Playing in this game has provided some unforgettable memories. The home run I hit in the 1984 All-Star Game at San Francisco was one of the top moments of my career.

I'm glad I had those moments from the 1980 season to reflect on, because 1981 was hardly an All-Star season for me. My batting average fell below .250, and my production dropped in just about every category. In fact, I was asked to take a cut in salary the following year. That's bad!

And then there was the players' strike. Without going into too much detail, the main issue was compensation for free agents moving from one team to another—whether clubs losing a free agent should be entitled to pick another player to compensate for that lost player. I didn't agree with that, and as assistant player representative for the Braves, I was indirectly involved with negotiations over the issue. I didn't feel baseball players ought to be tagged with restrictions not present in any other industry. But I really didn't want to see it go to a strike. I felt pretty crummy during the whole thing. It's not that I didn't agree with our point of view, but the only real losers during the strike were fans and cities—two groups that deserved much better treatment. I felt even worse when the second strike started in 1985. It was as if baseball hadn't learned its lesson. I was sure relieved when both strikes ended, and especially grateful the second one lasted only two days. Another long strike might have hurt the sport in ways it would never have recovered from.

I do think it's necessary to take a stand sometimes. Curt Flood, the player who first challenged free agency, and others put their necks on the line for my good. Because of it, baseball has never been better for players than today. I felt I had to stand up for the players of tomorrow. I wish it could have been done in another way, and I hope the sport will never have the threat of another strike. If we are fortunate, negotiations will bring the needed results from now on, and everyone will be willing to compromise a little.

As bad as 1981 was for my career, I still had a lot to be thankful for. I now had a family to come home to every day, and nothing on the baseball field could take them away from me. I had the gospel to raise my children in. I had as much security as the insecure world of baseball could offer. My first four years in the majors were pretty rocky at times, yet I could always see the hand of the Lord there to guide me to smoother waters, sometimes in ways that really surprised me.

I usually don't like to mix my baseball and family lives, but the annual Braves fathers and children's game at the stadium is an enjoyable exception. This one is in 1982 with Chad.

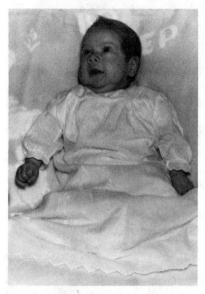

My goodness, was I ever this young?

Dad was always good about playing with Susan and me.

Mom brought out the gentler side in us, like here on Easter Day.

A summertime visit to the Murphy farm in Nebraska was always a lot of fun.

I usually wasn't as serious as I look here.

The first of many hobbies I've had through the years!

We always seemed to have plenty to smile and laugh about when I was growing up.

My baseball career began humbly — as a batboy for a team my father coached. I'm the little fellow in the front; Dad is the adult on the right.

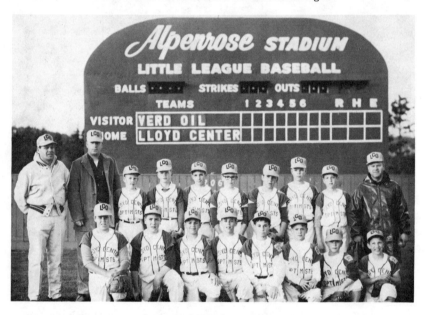

Now I've made the big time, getting to play at Alpenrose Dairy, the Yankee Stadium of Little League parks. I'm third from the right on the front row.

Maybe one reason why I chose baseball over football . . .

. . . is that it's much easier to keep the uniforms clean!

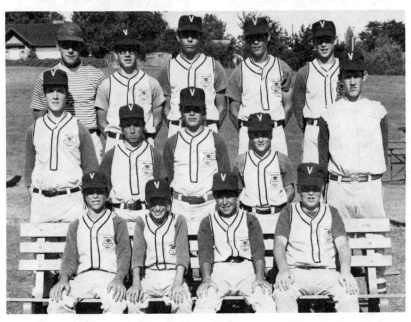

I'm finally getting tall enough to make the back row of team photos (far right). This is a Babe Ruth all-star team in Portland, 1969.

This is three years later in Richmond, Virginia, my last assignment in the minor leagues. By now I've already tasted major-league life — briefly.

If I look pretty young and green, it's because I'm a brand-new rookie at Kingsport, Tennessee, my first minor league stop.

Christmases at home (top) were always something special to a home-sick minor leaguer, and I couldn't wait this year to give Dad and Mom the chairs I picked up for them during my months in the Dominican Republic (above).

Barry and Stefnie Bonnell really made this day possible for me, and I'm grateful they were able to share it with us. (*Deseret News* photo)

I've had a lot of great experiences in my life, but none could top this.

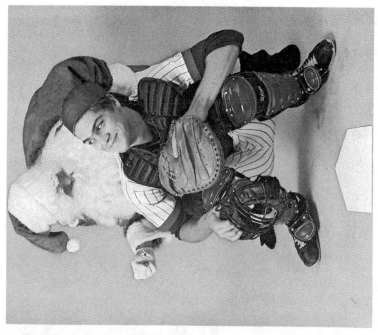

I'm told this 1979 Atlanta Braves Christmas Card could be a collector's item someday. I wasn't a catcher after this.

As a young major leaguer, I tried to keep my eyes and ears open and hustle, hustle, hustle.

Pittsburgh was a favorite stop during my first few years in the majors, because Dad and Mom lived there.

The greeting I get after hitting a home run is something I never get tired of.

Getting to rub shoulders (and elbows) with baseball's best players was the highlight of my first All-Star Game in 1980. I'm celebrating a National League win with Steve Garvey (left), Mario Soto (center), and Gary Carter. (UPI photo)

The final few moments before I bat are crucial. I need to get set just right in the batter's box, quickly survey how the defense is positioned, and review one more time how the pitcher is likely to throw to me.

Running the bases provides no time to relax. One quick move, and the pitcher can pick you off — and that's embarrassing!

When I'm not batting or in the field, I'll often study the game from the dugout.

Whenever the off-season routine of exercise and weight lifting gets a little boring (left), I try to think about how nice it feels to watch a well-hit ball fly toward the fence (right).

The on-deck circle is a good place to think, review, and psych yourself up.

A batting cage meeting with Pedro Guerrero, one of the finest players in the game.

Some runs come easy, some come hard. I barely miss Joe Niekro's tag to score here.

Meeting President Ronald Reagan in 1984 was a big thrill for me (left: AP/Wide World photo). So was meeting President Gordon B. Hinckley of my church's First Presidency (right: *Deseret News* photo).

I'm trying to do as little damage as possible to our kitchen — and stomachs. I enjoy cooking almost as much as eating.

Here's the Murphy clan, not long before Tyson, our fourth son, was born. Chad is seated. I'm holding Shawn, and Nancy is holding Travis.

Atlanta is a great city for family outings, and Stone Mountain (top) is one of our favorite places, but many times we just like to go and run around the park (above).

It's always nice to see people I know at the ballpark.

11 | The MVP Seasons

Each year before the baseball season, I sit down and set some goals for myself. I usually don't share them with other people, but I can tell you two things about my goal session before the 1982 season:

(1) I wasn't very happy with myself.

(2) Becoming the National League's Most Valuable Player wasn't anywhere on that list of goals, nor even in my wildest dreams.

How could it be? After the season I'd had in 1981, my thoughts were headed down an entirely different path. "Here you have been blessed with this athletic ability," I told myself, "and you're not using it. You're holding yourself back. It's about time you started doing what people have been saying you're capable of doing."

I felt an intense desire to rebound for several reasons. Of course, I had a family I was responsible for and I needed to provide for them. Also, the better I played, the more opportunities I'd have to share my religious beliefs with others—particularly through the media. That was a promise I had made to the Lord when we decided baseball would be my first mission field. By playing better I could serve him better.

Then, I'll admit, came personal pride. I wanted to prove I was a better ballplayer than I showed in 1981. I usually avoid this kind of motivation. If a player must have a bad year to motivate himself to have a good one, his career will move up and down like a yo-yo. My ultimate desire is to become consistent, but batting .247 (like I did in '81) is not the level of consistency I had in mind. The Braves' management had asked me to take the maximum possible twenty-percent salary cut after 1981, and there was a lot of publicity about that in the media during the off-season. I'd be dishonest if I said it doesn't hurt to see my failings detailed in public. But it made me all the more determined to prove I was a better player than many people then thought.

As you can see, these were hardly the thoughts of someone planning to win an MVP award. My career wasn't anywhere near that level. If you had told me that day that in several months I'd be asked to fly to New York to accept this great honor, well, first I would have laughed, and then I would have told you it would require a miracle greater than some of those miracles in the Bible.

After what happened to me in 1982, I think I learned one thing: Miracles still do happen!

The way our team started in 1982 was nothing short of miraculous. We won our first thirteen games, an all-time baseball record that may never be broken. To give you an idea how remarkable this streak was, consider this: A season in which a team wins sixty percent of its games is thought of as very successful (we would end this year winning just fifty-five percent of ours). If a team wins five games in a row, that is considered a major winning streak. And yet here we were, more than two weeks into the season without a single loss.

A long winning streak is always fun, but doubly so at the start of a season. It gets you off to a good start mentally. It helps the team gain confidence in itself right off. It generates an excitement that only a pennant race can match. Many people are glad to see baseball return each year—it's a reliable sign of spring, I guess. So when a team gets off to a big start, it captures the imagination of people all over the nation, especially when the team was not expected to do much. The media begins to analyze the streaking club. Is this the team of destiny this year? How long will the streak last? Will they win it all? People don't realize that even a record winning streak makes up just a tiny fraction of a 162-game season, and that many months of baseball, including some losing streaks, lie ahead.

But, hey, I wasn't about to let this fact of life keep me from getting caught up in the excitement as the streak continued. It was all very new to me—to most of us on the Braves, for that matter. As we got closer to the record for consecutive wins, it was like we were in the playoffs. A lot of fans were coming to see our games. Writers from all over wanted to see this new phenomenon called the Atlanta Braves. The streak was so much fun, it seems we were constantly telling each other, "Hey, let's keep this thing going one more day." It was like a snowball rolling down a hill, getting bigger and bigger and going faster and faster. Each game seemed bigger and more important than the one before.

When we finally broke the major-league record for consecutive wins at the start of a season, much of the pressure was off. But when you're riding a streak like this, you just want to keep it going and see how far it will take you. With each victory you're breaking new ground and making it that much harder for another team to come along later and take over your record. We were proud of that streak, though I think we tried to downplay its importance to the media to take some of the pressure off.

It's strange. The difference between winning thirteen in a row and losing eleven in a row (which we did later that same season) is not that much. Teams are usually competitive enough that a game's result might hinge on a few breaks. You get them, you win. You don't, you lose. Over the course of a season you do some of both, and it takes 162 games to see which team rises to the top. It's rare when one club is clearly better than the others. That's why you take these long winning streaks and ride them for all they're worth. You don't ever let up. The extra game or two you win during a streak may end up making the difference for a division championship. That's exactly what happened to us.

The streak finally ended with our fourteenth game. We came up against a hot pitcher, Bruce Berenyi of the Cincinnati Reds, I think, and lost a close game. There's always a little feeling of relief when something like this ends—now the entire nation wouldn't be watching the Atlanta Braves' every move. We could relax and just play our game. And after winning thirteen in a row, we were confident we had a pretty good game going. (We may have relaxed a bit too much — our team went on to lose four more games in a row.)

Luckily, I was off to an excellent start myself. It was sure nice to be able to bury those lingering doubts from the previous season. I was hitting for average *and* power now. And I finally felt comfortable in the outfield. It was the first time I could remember going out and just letting it happen. That was a nice experience, and I think it signaled the start of a new era in my career. I was named the National League Player of the Month for April, though I think the main reason for that was how the team, not I, was playing. Whatever the reasons, I'm sure you realize how meaningful this award was to me after my performance in 1981.

After both opening streaks, we started doing some winning and some losing — about the same of both. Even though our team had set a major league record for victories to start a season, we were never able to build a comfortable lead in our division. San Diego had also started well and was never more than a handful of games behind us through the first half of the year. And then there were those Los Angeles Dodgers; we figured we'd hear from them sooner or later. We were playing just well enough to maintain a lead in the division, but not well enough to make that lead comfortable.

And me? I was able to keep my batting average in the .290 to .310 range, with enough home runs and RBI to keep things pleasant. What made me the happiest, though, was that I'd finally seemed to find the consistency I'd been searching for. There were no major streaks after April, but no big slumps, either.

In July our team started to break loose again. We weren't winning all of our games, but enough to gradually widen the lead over San Diego and the Dodgers. By the end of the month, we were in first place by about ten games. In baseball that's a healthy margin.

Speaking of breaking loose, my nose did exactly that in a Sunday afternoon game at Chicago. On the last play of the game, a pop fly was hit between me and our shortstop, Rafael Ramirez. He backed up as I charged in, and we got to the ball at the same time. My nose smashed into the back of his head. Rafael caught the ball and we won the game, but I had a painful, bloody mess in the middle of my face. A doctor examined it and found that I had broken a small bone in my nose. But being in a pennant race does funny things to people, and all I wanted to know was whether I could still play the following night. This was nothing like my knee injury; you don't run on your nose, after all. And since they've never conducted a beauty pageant in the major leagues, I didn't have to worry about that. It hurt like crazy, but as long as I could breathe, I wanted to play. The team was doing well, I was doing well, and I didn't want to miss a minute of Atlanta's first divisional championship in almost fifteen years. The doctor told me that if I took it easy for twenty-four hours, there was a chance I could play the next night. Never have I followed a doctor's instructions so faithfully. And though I wasn't a pretty sight, I did get to play Monday night.

A lot of good things were happening to our team—and to me. My average was now near .310, and I was leading the league in home runs and runs batted in. For the first time I had been chosen by fans to start for the National League at the All-Star Game, an honor that absolutely thrilled me. Unlike in 1980, I thought maybe I had played well enough this year to belong there. And I felt pretty good about my defense. After playing all three outfield positions in the first month of the season, I had settled into center field. It was nice to finally have a place to call my own.

Why did things turn around so quickly? I'd always thought there was a better player hidden inside me and maybe I just needed to mature enough in the majors for him to come out. Also, I was a little more determined and intense after what happened in 1981.

But there's something else that really helped me, and it's never been mentioned very much. That something was Joe Torre. 1982 was Joe's first year as our manager, and he brought a lot to the team. I don't say this to discredit Bobby Cox, our manager before Joe. Bobby was a great manager, as he proved when he went to the Toronto Blue Jays and helped turn them into one of baseball's best teams in just a few years. As you remember, he may also have been responsible for saving my career by moving me to the outfield. He was always great to play for, and I'm glad he returned to the Braves before the 1986 season as our general manager. But having Joe here was one of those cases when the right person came along at just the right time.

Joe took me under his wing. In some ways I'm the same kind of hitter he was—some power, not a lot of speed, and a need to make contact consistently to help the team. Joe worked with

me a lot on my batting stance and hitting style. He wanted me
to hit to the opposite field more. Without getting too technical, I
hope, here's how it works: Many power hitters tend to "pull"
the ball. For a right-handed hitter like me, that means I usually
hit the ball to left field. You can often hit with more power that
way—your arms are more extended, and you get better leverage to hit the ball long and hard. But pulling also has its disad-
vantages. Most pull hitters end up with a lower batting average;
they're easier to defend because you can better predict where
they'll hit the ball. A good pitcher can usually throw the ball
away from a pull hitter's strengths. That leaves many of these
hitters depending on pitchers' mistakes and the occasional
lucky pitch where the bat meets the ball just right.

Joe wanted me to hit to the whole field. He tried to convince
me I could hit home runs to right and center field as often as to
left field. I didn't believe him at first, but he was right. About
75 percent of my home runs were *not* hit to left field in 1982.
"Just go with the pitch," Joe would always tell me. Hey, I
was listening. As a hitter, Joe had proved he could put it together for an entire season. He hit .360 one year (now, *that's* an
incredible year!) and was named the league's Most Valuable
Player. His lifetime average was near that magic .300 level—all
this while catching, too. So when Joe talked hitting, I listened. I
backed away from the plate so I could better hit inside pitches
(that's where pitchers were consistently getting me out), and I
became more selective, learning to wait for the pitch *I* wanted. If
it didn't come, I took a base on balls. Joe talked to me constantly about how to think at the plate. It all added up to a
smarter hitter who was a little tougher to pitch to and harder to
defend. Thanks, Joe.

He helped the rest of the team, too. When we were on our
way to that 13-0 start, he kept us from getting too starry-eyed.
He always preached the same thing: Play with your head as well
as your body, be aggressive, and don't take anything for
granted. That one easy ground ball you hit but then don't hustle
on because you think you've just become an easy out, may be
the one the shortstop bobbles. Joe kept his wits about him even
when we went into that horrible slump in August, lost nineteen
of twenty-one games, and tumbled into second place.

Oh, yes, THE slump. I was afraid we'd get to that sooner or
later. The best instruction from the best teacher still doesn't
make you slump-proof. In case you're wondering, going 2-19,

including losing eleven in a row is just about as unusual as winning thirteen straight. I don't ever remember another team going through a slump like we did—and still winning the title. But that lead we had built in July was sort of our "year's supply," and it saved us from getting booted out of the pennant race altogether.

I certainly did more than my fair share to keep the slump going. My batting average fell about twenty-five points (a lot for that time of year) in three weeks. I virtually stopped driving people in and hitting home runs, and Joe nearly benched me a couple of times. It was mighty frustrating. Remember how I described the feelings of a team on a long winning streak? Just the opposite feelings take over in a losing streak, especially when you're on top of the division and fighting to stay there. It seemed that almost every morning I'd wake up to see our lead in the standings shrink by a game. Then one morning we were in second place. We weren't so anxious to go to the ballpark then. Nerves were on edge a little more. We wondered what would go wrong with us that day. Pressure mounted as the streak got longer, and sometimes arguments broke out among team-mates. Thanks to Joe, we managed to stay as calm as might be expected during that three-week ordeal. It would have been easy for the team to disintegrate for the rest of the season after a streak like that.

But we were still awfully frustrated as the losses piled up, particularly since eight of them went to the Dodgers, a team we had developed a rivalry with, but who was now rapidly catching —and passing—us.

Going through a personal slump at the same time as the team's slump makes it twice as tough. You can take at least some comfort when you're having problems but the team is winning. If you want to be fascinated sometime, study a player or a team in a slump. Watch how they react. Some will just go along naturally, figuring they'll eventually work their way out of it. But some will try *anything* to end it.

I've never been very superstitious—I joke that the only superstition I have is to touch first base when I'm running the bases. But some players go to great lengths to find a key to end their slump. They'll eat certain foods or wear certain clothes or do things in a certain order. A shortstop I played with in the minors was having defensive problems, so he brought a sleeping bag to the ballpark and slept at his position. It helped.

Another pitcher I know got batted around pretty good one inning, so he drop-kicked his mitt as he walked back to the dugout. The next inning he set the other team down with no trouble. From then on he drop-kicked his mitt into the dugout after each inning.

Sometimes, even whole teams can get involved. The 1982 Braves were involved in one of the most famous superstitious incidents in baseball history. The club had a mascot named Chief Noc-a-Homa who had a tepee set up on a platform behind the outfield fence. The chief performed Indian dances during games—special ones to jinx our opponents, a rain dance for early innings when we were behind, and a war dance after one of our players hit a home run. He was pretty popular with the fans, but when the pennant race heated up in 1982, the Braves' management decided to take the chief's tepee out and install more seats in its place.

You guessed it. Right after they did that, we went into our big 2-19 slump. I felt it was a coincidence, but a lot of people, including some of our players, said there was a jinx or a curse on the team. I must admit that as our losing streak got longer and longer, I began to wonder myself. Anyway, there was such an uproar from our fans all over the country that the club finally decided to put Chief Noc-a-Homa back in his original home. We started to win again soon after that.

Athletes in slumps are desperate people, and they some- times resort to some pretty outlandish things to deal with them. There's also the temptation to mess with some pretty basic things—a different stance, new bat, different grip. Advice is free, and you get plenty of it while in a slump. You tend to dis- count most of it. You'd go crazy if you didn't. I could write a book just about the things I've been told to do to end a slump. You wouldn't believe some of them, though they come from people who are well meaning and only want to help.

But whenever I want to totally shut myself off from such advice, I hear a story like John Tudor's or Keith Hernandez's. John, a pitcher for the St. Louis Cardinals, got off to a terrible start in 1985. He won maybe only one of his first seven deci- sions. Then a college teammate told him he'd seen him on TV and noted that his pitching delivery had changed since he'd known him. It was only a minor alteration, but John took it to heart and lost just one game for the rest of the season! Keith Hernandez's father was watching him on a satellite system

Keith just had installed for him. Keith wasn't hitting too well at the time, and his father quickly spotted why. When he had been hitting normally, his father told him, he could see the entire number on his back from the center field TV camera. Now he could see just part of it. Keith adjusted and immediately went on a hitting tear, almost leading the New York Mets to a pennant.

Usually, though, what a slumping player wants is peace and quiet, with maybe a few words of advice from a hitting instructor or manager. The best attribute for someone in a slump, they say, is a bad memory. Sometimes the reaction to a slump is worse than the slump itself. I don't believe in shutting myself off from the world whenever I'm in one. So that means I'll read about it and hear about it. Even if I were to go into a shell, there would be the unavoidable reminders, like the one I get from Chad every so often: "You didn't hit a home run again tonight, did you, Daddy?"

The best solution, I suppose, is not to have slumps. Now if any of you out there have the answer to that, I'd be glad to listen! Slumps are just as inevitable as colds, and because I'm a streaky hitter I'll probably always have more than my share. I only hope I'll always handle them in a dignified way.

Every player in the major leagues can gratefully tell you one thing: Slumps eventually come to an end. Mine did, and so did the Braves'. But now, rather than coasting along with a ten-game lead, we were four games behind the Dodgers, and the San Francisco Giants were rapidly closing in.

September 1982 was a strange month. A team will usually take control down the stretch and win the pennant in that final full month of the season. But the Braves, Dodgers, and Padres took turns beating up on each other, winning about as many as they lost. Only the Giants were hot, and they came closer and closer through September. Had the season been one week longer, the Giants might well have won the pennant.

Some writers were calling it the title no one wanted. We wanted it, and wanted it very badly. But so did the other teams. Maybe that's why we kept beating each other. But I'll tell you, playing in a pennant race was like nothing else I'd ever experienced. I came to the ballpark every day with a feeling that this would be the most important game of the season.

There were always two games—one on the field and one going on elsewhere, but flashed on the scoreboard. I've never seen a team that doesn't closely watch the scoreboard during a pennant race. You wait anxiously for each bit of news from the other games. When the "good guys" score a run, you feel a lift. When the "bad guys" do, you feel a little deflated. But often you don't even have to turn and look at the scoreboard — just listening to the crowd will give you an accurate indication of how things are going. Everything is magnified during a pennant race: the crowds, the runs, the big defensive plays, the mistakes. It makes what is already a great game just that much more fun.

Our race came down to the final day, as we suspected it would. We were in San Diego, and the Dodgers were in San Francisco. We blew our chance to clinch the title by losing 5-1 to the Padres. Then we had to watch, in agony, for more than half an hour as the Dodgers and Giants finished their game. A Los Angeles win would have tied the division and forced a one-game playoff at Dodger Stadium. With the luck we'd had lately against the Dodgers, that prospect didn't interest us. It was a close game, I remember, when the Giants' Joe Morgan stepped up and hit a three-run home run that ended up winning it. Joe Morgan for President? We were all for it. The Braves could finally celebrate winning a division title, though surviving was what we'd really done. (In our defense, though, we did win five of our final seven games, when it really counted, all on the West Coast.) But the title meant the same whether we won it by one game or ten, so we proudly headed to St. Louis to play the Cardinals for the right to go to the World Series.

World Series — those words send chills down nearly every baseball player's spine. It's the ultimate thrill. I'll bet 95 percent of the players would trade in every individual honor they'd ever win for a World Series ring. I'm one of them. But to get there, we'd first have to win three playoff games before the Cardinals could, and that wouldn't be easy.

I thought the pennant race was great, but it was nothing compared to the playoffs. It's funny what sticks out in my mind about them now. I remember looking up at the scoreboard and seeing only St. Louis versus Atlanta and Milwaukee versus California (the American League playoff series) up there. It hit me — hey, we're the only ones left! Then you think of the millions and millions of people watching you that very moment. I hope my cap was on straight.

We got off to a good start that quickly turned sour. Phil Niekro was pitching a great first game, and we were leading 1-0 going into the bottom of the fifth inning. Then a big thunderstorm hit. Was that ever bad timing! The Cardinals had to bat only one more time for the game to become an official win for us, then it could rain all it wanted as far as we were concerned. The officials ended up postponing the game, which caused quite a bit of controversy. We felt if they had waited long enough, they could have restarted the game at least long enough to make it official. But I guess TV networks don't like to sit through long rain delays, so it was decided to call the game. We were within three outs of possibly winning the first playoff game, and then suddenly we were told we'd have to start all over the next day. The team was pretty dejected in the clubhouse afterwards. It's a good thing we didn't know then that this had been the first rainout at Busch Stadium in more than six years!

We wished the next day's game had been rained out, too. The Cardinals won, 7-0. After still another rainout the following day, we seemed to come back stronger for Game 2. Phil was pitching again, and we had a 3-1 lead by the middle of the game. But the Cards kept chipping away at us and won 4-3, scoring a run in the bottom of the ninth inning.

We were down two games to none, but at least we were returning to Atlanta for as many as three more games. We were hoping for a big, enthusiastic crowd to cheer us on. The crowd was there, all right, but St. Louis scored four runs early in the game and we could never catch up. They won, 6-2, clinching the series in a 3-0 sweep.

The Cardinals were off to the World Series (which they won), and we were off for home. It'd be easy to make the excuse that the first rainout, when we easily could have won, was the reason for our downfall. It wasn't, though. The Cardinals were clearly the better team and deserved all the success that came to them. I was disappointed in being swept like that and especially disappointed in my own performance. (I managed only three singles, and an important rally might have ended when I was caught trying to steal third base in Game 2.) But I wasn't disappointed in the playoffs. It was a marvelous and exciting experience.

I wish I could say a quiet winter followed, but that's not the way it turned out. There had been a lot of talk in the media about my being the leading candidate for the National League's Most Valuable Player award. Frankly, I was a little embarrassed by that. Sure, the statistics I had were the best of my career. But it usually takes more than 36 home runs and 109 RBI and much more than a .281 batting average to win the award. And if my August slump weren't enough to eliminate me from contention, there was one more big slump I haven't even mentioned yet.

From the middle of September through the end of the season, I didn't do much at all with my bat to help the team. They managed to win the division title in spite of me, not because of me. Everyone was quick to make excuses on my behalf. They pointed out that Bob Horner was injured at about the same time I went into my slump and that not having him behind me in the lineup made it a lot tougher for me to hit. I'll admit that pitchers were able to throw a little more carefully to me because they didn't have to worry about Bob's powerful bat. But I don't think it was that great a factor. Bob has never swung my bat for me. And I don't always go into a slump when he's injured. It was, pure and simple, a slump. I just wasn't swinging well. It took some of the joy away from what had been a good year for me, because I felt I had let the team down when they needed me most.

Joe Torre has never been one to let statistics speak for themselves. He had watched me hit, or try to hit, for the last three weeks of the season. "You've lost your hitting zone, Murph," he finally told me after the playoffs ended. So even though he might have just looked at my numbers and passed it off as a good year, he knew something had to be done. After our final loss to St. Louis, he invited me to go to "hitting school" with him down in Florida. It surprised me at first, but when I realized I could combine this with a trip to Disney World for my family, I jumped at the chance. Joe spent five days with me in batting practices and "skull sessions." We talked hitting for hours — the philosophy, mental approach, and maybe the toughest thing of all: hitting curve balls! Joe gave me plenty to think about over the winter and again made me a little smarter hitter. The more I've thought about it, the more grateful I am to Joe for consistently going the extra mile. It was truly a selfless gesture for him to take time from his own off-season to work with me.

Many laughed at the irony of an MVP candidate going back to "hitting school." But Joe and I both knew that I was still too prone to streaks and slumps, and I had a lot to learn before I could become a pure hitter.

So after these two slumps and my little schooling session, I was still surprised at being considered MVP material. When the media called and asked me what I thought about it, I told them the honest truth. I told them that I thought Al Oliver of Montreal, Lonnie Smith of St. Louis, or Pedro Guerrero of Los Angeles deserved it more than I did. And I meant it. Overall I'd had a good season, but not the great one you usually associate with this award.

Still, as weeks went by, it looked like I'd be among the top vote-getters. So when the call came from New York telling me I'd won the MVP, I wasn't shocked, but I was still a little surprised. It was a nice experience to go and accept the award, but I'll be the first to admit I wasn't an overwhelming choice or that my statistics weren't of traditional MVP caliber.

Remember the miracle I was talking about earlier? Well, the circumstances behind this award could just about qualify as one. First of all, no one in the league had eye-popping statistics. Just about every year someone manages to put up some big numbers. No one did this year, except maybe Al Oliver.

But Al wasn't fortunate enough to play on a division-winning team. If he had, he'd have won it easily. They call the MVP an individual award, but so much depends on others: teammates getting on base so you can drive them in, your team winning, coaches working with and encouraging you. Our *team* won the division. If they hadn't, there's no way I would have won the MVP. (This was a team, by the way, that was figured by nearly every baseball expert to finish in the middle of our division. Our title was a little miracle in itself. We had nearly every player back from a team that had lost more games than it won in 1981. And only one of our original starting pitchers was still healthy at the end of the year.)

I've never felt comfortable saying, "Hey, look what I've done," because I never feel like *I* did it. *I* had better statistics in 1985, but our team didn't do well, so I finished way back in the MVP voting. For some reason, I did win the MVP in 1982. I wanted to help the Lord and help others, but this wasn't exactly the way I thought it would come about. I don't believe the Lord says that because I have these desires, I will win an MVP award. But maybe he did in this case. It's a good possibility, because there were just too many far-fetched circumstances involved. Now, I don't mean this will happen to everyone. There are a lot of members of the Church with greater desires who live better lives than I do and work harder at their jobs. But they still may not get the promotion or reward they wish for.

Far be it from me to try to sort out the whys and hows. I remembered I had made a promise with the Lord and felt that I'd better live up to my end of the covenant. Winning the MVP did provide more opportunities to speak at banquets and meet with media around the nation. And though I didn't force the Church on others, it always seemed that conversations would turn to my religion. I was proud to tell everyone what a positive and significant role the gospel played in my life.

One award coming my way that did totally shock me was a Gold Glove, which honors defensive excellence. Receiving this award taught me something: If you work hard enough you can succeed, even if you end up doing something totally different from what you originally planned. It's a lesson that's helped me in many areas of my life.

It was a busy off-season in other ways, too. Our third son, Shawn, was born in December, completing our first little outfield. And I was faced with a major contract negotiation before the 1983 season began.

I get a little uncomfortable when talking about money. I'd just as soon go out and play and never have to worry about it. But it's a fact of life, so we prepared to meet with the Braves. I had sat in on a negotiating session a few years before and didn't enjoy it at all, so I asked my agent to handle the whole thing this time. Bruce Church is his name, and I like him because he's low-key and doesn't try to grab headlines. What I really wanted was security for my family and enough to be able to really help the Church. I told Bruce only to be fair and honest. When he came back with his proposal, I nearly choked. But he convinced me that it was not only a fair request, but the going rate for a player of my experience, ability, and potential; so I told him to go ahead.

Not too much later we signed a contract that would pay me about $8 million to play for the Braves for the next five years. I realize we don't provide the services of a doctor, a fireman, or a teacher, and yet we are paid so much more. But it would have been unfair to my family, the Lord, and myself to agree to less than was fair at that time.

I also have strong feelings about the violation of contracts. Once the paper is signed, it should be stuck to. Some players figure they're worth more than they're being paid in the middle of their contract, so they'll withhold their services until its renegotiated. Players have their eyes wide open when they sign contracts, and if it doesn't end up working in their favor, that's a mistake they ought to live with. You never see teams paying their players less money because they don't perform to the level of their contracts. And yet you see plenty of players breaking their contracts to demand more money. I just don't think that's right.

Now I had a contract that would expect an awful lot from me. And I was determined to give the Braves their money's worth.

The new contract wasn't my only source of pressure as we started the 1983 season. Many more sets of eyes were focused on me to see if my MVP award was really a fluke. Spring training was a lot busier than usual, but I think Joe's post-season hitting seminar in Florida helped prepare me better than ever for opening day. I had lost my confidence at the end of '82, and without Joe's help I might have gone into the season with that same feeling. Instead, I felt ready and confident that I could become a more consistent hitter. MVP or no MVP, I had a lot to prove in that way.

We lost on opening day, which meant no winning-streak record this year. But then we turned around and won our next seven in a row, and our record after sixteen games was 13-3, exactly the same as in 1982. We were off to another great start, but so were the Dodgers.

For the next three months we lived in each other's shadows in the standings. For about two of those months, our teams had the best records of the twenty-six clubs in baseball. Then, just as in 1982, we put together a good July while the Dodgers slumped. By the middle of August we had a solid seven-game lead over them. Pennant fever again hit Atlanta. The stadium filled up once more (though they didn't dare take Chief Noc-a-Homa's tepee out this time!), and each game grew more and more important.

Unfortunately, we lost the lead just about as quickly as we had the year before. We were losing about two-thirds of our games, while the Dodgers began winning almost all of theirs.

Before the end of August we had fallen to second place. Bob
Horner was again lost to the team because of injury for the rest
of the year, right about the time we started our skid. We
obviously missed him down the stretch, and though we put
together little rallies in the final month, we just couldn't win
consistently enough to overtake the Dodgers. Los Angeles elimi-
nated us two games before the season ended. I'll tell you, it was
a strange, empty feeling going to the stadium those last two
days after having every ballgame in the past few years mean so
much to the team.

From our opening streak in 1982 to the Dodgers' finally
clinching the pennant in 1983, there was an intensity and excitement I'd never experienced before in baseball. Sure, there
were big games in high school and in the minors, but they were
without the large, packed stadiums, widespread media coverage, and nationwide attention. In my earlier years in the majors,
the Braves were realistically out of the pennant race with a
month or two to go. Having been on both sides of the race, I can
tell you it's many times more fun being in it than out of it, even
though the pressure is also much greater. I've been in two real
pennant races now, and I'd enjoy many more—one a year
would be just fine.

So our team barely lost the title in 1983 after barely winning
it in 1982. Over the 162-game season, we'd lost just one more
game than in '82. When you come so close, you do a lot of thinking later about the hard-luck losses that might have made a
difference in the race.

There's one in particular that a lot of us on the Braves
thought about over and over that winter. We were making our
final trip to Los Angeles in the middle of September. Our team
went in just two games behind the Dodgers and knew we'd
leave anywhere from one game ahead to five games behind.
Needless to say, it was our biggest series of the year. We lost a
tough one-run game in the opener, but then came back to win in
ten innings the next night. Now, the final game of this series
would decide if we'd have one or three games to make up in the
final three weeks. You don't have to be a mathematician to
figure that it's three times as easy to make up one game as
three. It looked like we'd get things the easy way, for we led 6-3
going into the bottom of the ninth inning. With our relief
pitchers, that's as close to a sure thing as you can get. Well, the
roof fell in. The Dodgers quickly scored three runs, then won the

game on a suicide squeeze bunt. Our players stood there
stunned—it had all happened so fast. I don't think we recovered
from the shock, for then we went on to lose two in a row at Cincinnati, the last-place team in our division. This was while the
Dodgers were winning two out of three at Houston, and that
pretty well put us away—morale-wise, if not statistically.

While we suffered through nightmares of suicide squeezes in
the off-season, I also had a chance to evaluate my own performance, and I can honestly say I felt much better about it this
time around. It had easily been the most consistent season
among my first six years in the majors. Only one category
dropped from 1982—strikeouts. I tried not to let that bother me
too much! I did go through a one-month stretch when home
runs were pretty scarce, but I was still getting some other hits. I
didn't suffer through any of those long, deep slumps I'd always
been prone to in past years. Unlike in 1982, September '83
was a good month for me, which left a better taste in my mouth
after the season.

Again, much of this I credit to Joe Torre, who still worked
with me often. And you can't forget your teammates. Taking
full credit for statistics is foolish. Imagine Walter Payton feeling
he could gain those thousands of yards running the football on
his own. It's impossible. For me to drive in as many runs as I did
in 1983 (121) or, especially, to score 131 runs requires a good
hitting *team* around you. And we had one. In fact, the Braves
led the league in batting average and runs scored in '83. Those
are the kinds of things personal statistics are built on.

And, quite honestly, I should have been a better player than
I was in '82. I was a year older. I had had another year to learn
from my mistakes. It would have been really disappointing if I
had not improved in at least a few areas. But things came
together awfully well for me in 1983—much better than I
expected. So when people began talking about a possible
second MVP award after the season was over, I wasn't surprised
—nor embarrassed as I was in 1982.

What did embarrass me, though, was a series of articles,
particularly in the Atlanta newspapers, about my becoming
"the most complete player in baseball today." Personally, I
wasn't about to buy that. Here I'd enjoyed two good seasons,
and they were ready to put a Superman cape on me instead of a
Braves' uniform. It really did embarrass me. For some time
there was a running argument in the papers whether Dale

Murphy or André Dawson or someone else was the best player in baseball. I didn't want any part of it.

I sought out Johnny Bench one day, told him how I felt, and asked him for advice. "Just keep telling them that André Dawson is the best player you've ever seen," Johnny told me. "That will really stump them." I pretty well did that, but that still didn't explain my embarrassment at even being included in this debate.

I had been in the major leagues for six full years, and only three of those were what I would call "good" ones. I still struck out too much and had too many slumps. I played at a relatively undemanding position that I was still learning. What about Cal Ripken, Jr.? He plays one of the toughest positions (shortstop) and still puts up MVP-caliber numbers almost every year. Or Don Mattingly? or Dave Winfield? or Pedro Guerrero? or André Dawson? or Jim Rice? or George Brett? or Keith Hernandez? or Pete Rose? These guys have done it just about every season they've been in the majors. The fact I've had a few more "good" seasons doesn't change that fact. I still strike out too much. I still make dumb mistakes in the field. I still need to become more consistent. And even if I thought the term *most complete player* might fit someday, which I doubt, I'd still feel the same way I did after 1983. My teammates get on base so I can drive them in; my teammates drive me in; my coaches give me instruction that helps me go out and play better. My part in anything I do depends so much on other people.

An MVP award, even two MVP awards in a row, does not automatically make someone the best player around. It made me the right person in the right place at the right time. As I said before, I felt I had a better season in 1985 than 1982, yet finished way back in the MVP voting. The team just didn't do very well in 1985. That's why I thought my chances to win the MVP in '83 were not as good. Mike Schmidt of the Phillies and the Dodgers' Pedro Guerrero both had great seasons and were on championship-winning teams, just as I was in 1982. André Dawson had also enjoyed another super season.

Yet, for some reason I received the same phone call from New York telling me I'd won the award again. I wasn't embarrassed this year, only humbled and grateful that the Lord had blessed me with so much. If I could have seen five years before what was going to happen to me, I would have laughed it off as an impossible dream. I didn't even think I'd stay in the minors, let alone the big leagues. After all the obstacles in my first few years in the majors, I felt fortunate just to be playing. So how could I do anything but credit the Lord for these things?

We celebrated this second MVP award as we do all other special occasions in our family—we went out to eat. Everyone kept asking me how I felt, and I didn't really know what to tell them other than "fine." I don't think I'll be able to express what these things mean to me until my career is over and I can look back on everything in perspective.

One thing that worried me: I didn't want anyone to treat me differently or put me on a higher level just because I happened to win some individual awards. I just wanted people to treat me like the regular guy I was. Besides, things always seem to happen in life that make you realize how small even an MVP award stacks up. Nancy lost a baby in the fourth month of pregnancy during the summer. And Travis continued to suffer from health difficulties that eventually led to a serious bout with pneumonia. At any time I would have traded those MVP trophies and all they represented to have that little spirit alive in our home and to be blessed with Travis's health.

Don't misunderstand me. I'm not discounting the importance of the awards. They mean a lot to me. But not nearly as much as becoming an MVP to my wife, my children, and the Lord. Know what else? I'd even trade both trophies in for something else I don't have right now—a World Series ring!

I learned an important lesson in 1983 that I hope might help you as it helped me.

Early in my career I was somewhat limited in the things I felt I could do to help our team. I thought that calling good, intelligent games as a catcher, playing that position well defensively, and hitting for a decent average were all the team should expect from me. Of course, we all know what happened there. As I learned new positions, I felt it gave me a temporary excuse for my bat not to be as strong as it could be.

But as time went on, I began to recognize this for what it was—a cop-out. I realized my only limitations were those I placed on myself. Something my dad used to tell me suddenly gained new meaning: "Dare to be good." He's right. Sometimes it requires extra effort, some risks, even quite a bit of daring to be good at something.

I decided that hitting home runs and playing the outfield

well were just some of the things I could do to help the team. I started searching and discovered I was able to do a few things I never thought I could.

Probably the most surprising was stealing bases. I had never tried to steal many bases, because I had told myself I wouldn't be good at it. I had placed that limitation on myself. There were pretty good reasons for doing this. I'm a big fellow, and my speed can best be described as average among major leaguers. But in listening to the great base stealers, I found one thing mentioned most often: Few bases were stolen by sheer speed. Most of their success came through studying pitchers' motions, getting just the right lead and jump, and knowing how to slide into second base to miss the tag.

I began spending some time during games studying these things. And I began to experiment with it myself. My stolen base totals went from 6 in 1979 to 30 in 1983. That total in '83 was especially significant to me. Only five other players in major league history had hit at least 30 home runs while also stealing 30 or more bases: Bobby Bonds, Hank Aaron, Willie Mays, Tommy Harper, and Ken Williams. That was pretty humbling company. I don't say this to boast, and I hope you don't think I am. I just want to make this point: When I told myself I couldn't steal bases, I didn't. When I began to honestly work at it, I found some abilities I never knew I had. Now that doesn't mean everything I've tried like this has become a great success. But how many times do we automatically say we aren't good at math, or at writing, or at stolen bases, or anything else, without being willing to give it a good try? I've found in looking back that the greatest limitations I've ever had are those I placed on myself.

That philosophy has had a big impact on my traditional goal-setting sessions before each baseball season (and on my goal-setting in life, for that matter). It's helped me to set broader and more complete objectives to better gauge my performance after the season is over.

No, it didn't help me win two MVP awards.

12 Nowhere to Go but Down

It was August of 1984, and the Dodgers were in Atlanta to play us. The game was in the bottom of the ninth inning, with our potential tying run on third base and Ken Howell, a hard-throwing rookie, pitching for the Dodgers. I was especially eager to go up and hit. This had been a rough year for me in pressure situations, and I wanted to prove that the team could still count on me in the clutch.

I struck out.

Several months of frustration had built up, and I was about to vent it in a way I wasn't very proud of afterwards. When I got back to the dugout, I wiped out the plastic water cooler with one big kick. I didn't even have to look at the stunned expressions on my teammates' faces to realize what I'd just done. Normally mild-mannered Dale Murphy really lost his cool, and it made the headlines along with our loss the next day.

My career dropped into another valley in 1984, but this time it took my whole life along with it. I was just plain unhappy, and damaging myself every bit as much as I did that water cooler.

Though I'm certainly not proud of how I reacted to that strikeout, it did help in one way — it woke me up. I had allowed the game to consume me and also get in the way of my family. I remember Elder Paul Dunn warning me once that there would be people who would try to get me to put baseball ahead of other, more important things in my life. "Oh no," I thought, "I'll never let that happen," and yet I realized that, almost without thinking, I had let it happen. I had allowed the success I'd had in 1982 and 1983 to take me away from my family too much. And my desire to continue enjoying that success had begun to affect the way I acted.

Nancy was a tremendous help to me through this whole ordeal. She seemed to know when to comfort me after a bad night and when I needed a little reminder. My behavior after that game with the Dodgers called for one of those little reminders. "Look what you're doing to yourself," she told me. "If you're this unhappy, why don't you just quit?"

I told her I felt like quitting, but I knew that would be impossible. It wouldn't be right. Besides, I was under contract, and you've already read how I feel about contracts. I'd just have to change *my* ways somehow.

As I thought about it, everything boiled down to priorities. I had allowed mine to become misplaced. That's why I was so miserable and why my life seemed out of whack. As a matter of fact, I learned so much about priorities from these experiences, I've included a whole chapter about them later in this book. But in a nutshell, here's what I decided: First, I wasn't going to allow my baseball life to get in the way of my family life, even if I had to say no sometimes, which has always been hard for me to do. And second, I was going to enjoy my work more and not let performance become such a life-and-death matter to me. Even when your game hits a rough stretch, there is much to like about playing baseball.

Maybe after the two MVP awards I needed to be brought back down to earth. The 1984 season certainly did that.

When I flew to New York to accept a second MVP award in November 1983, I had no idea of the attention that would follow it. Things hadn't been that different for me after I received the first award in 1982. I hadn't been an overwhelming choice and had sort of come out of nowhere to win it. Everyone was probably still figuring out how to spell my name. But life became much busier in the first month of the off-season after 1983 — even before my winning the MVP was announced.

That second award brought more of everything. There were more speeches, more banquets, and more appearances all over the country. I was flattered to be invited to so many places and willingly accepted my new role in baseball. I figured doing all these things was part of the obligation of an MVP-award winner. I also figured, as I mentioned earlier, that it was my duty to the Lord to participate in as many of these functions as I could.

After a few more hectic months, I realized I had allowed myself to gradually cross that fine line that separates my family from baseball. I found it more and more difficult to spend enough time with Nancy and the boys. Even when I was home, I wasn't always able to divide my baseball life from my family life. Worse yet, this was taking place during the off-season, when players have the chance to make up for all the travel during the busy months of the baseball season by being with their families more.

This sort of attention was all very new to me, and I guess I had to learn the hard way how to handle it. I began to look forward to spring training as a chance to get both my game and my thoughts sorted out. I knew I'd have to make some rather unpleasant decisions to get the scales back in balance again.

But a different sort of attention waited for me in Florida. Almost from the moment we arrived in late February, talk of my winning a third straight MVP award began. No National League player had ever received it three times in a row. I really didn't plan on being the first. So much has to fall into place to receive an MVP. It's a subjective award. And it's possible to have a great season and not win it. It's not that I'm pessimistic, but it's just never in my goals or plans because there's so much associated with it that's out of my control.

Yet before I had even swung a bat at spring training, I'd answered dozens of times what I felt the likelihood was of my winning the award again. Pretty soon I began reading stories full of quotes from other players evaluating my chances. The first pitch of the exhibition season hadn't even been thrown yet, and it was like I was *supposed* to win the MVP again. I really couldn't blame the media. I guess this was to them a pretty obvious thing to watch for in the coming season, so it had to be reported on.

Again, all this attention was new to me. I'd never experienced anything like it earlier in my career. Maybe if I had played in a larger media market like New York, Chicago, or Los Angeles

I'd have been used to it. But suddenly there were a lot of reporters in the Braves' camp and a lot of interviews. Naturally,
the main reason they were talking to me was that the possibility
of a third consecutive MVP award was there. Often they would
point out that National League history was at stake—no one
had won it three times in a row; only Mike Schmidt, Ernie
Banks, and Joe Morgan had won it twice in a row; only Stan
Musial and Roy Campanella had won it three times in a career.
"Now, Dale, what are your chances of doing this?" They had to
be a little disappointed in my usual answer. It went something
like, "I'd love to win it, but I'd rather win a world championship."

That's truly how I felt. It'd be a nice award to win, but I
wasn't planning on it, nor would I lose sleep over it. I'd much
rather win a World Series title with my team.

Well, these many interviews translated into a lot of stories.
And not being one to avoid what is written or said in the media,
I saw my share of them. I had tried to keep all of this MVP
business out of my mind, but I'm afraid I ended up getting a
little too caught up in the whole thing. In addition to the
external pressure that's always on me to play well, I also put a
lot of pressure on myself. It was apparent that others were expecting another MVP from me. Maybe I began to expect the
same, afraid that anything less would disappoint a lot of people.

This all added up to an interesting experience at spring
training. I'm afraid my inability to say no sometimes hurt me a
little. Though I played pretty well in exhibition games, I wasn't
concentrating like I should. I let all the MVP-centered questions
turn my thoughts in that direction rather than to the proper
aspects of the team and game. Because I didn't say no when I
needed to or didn't organize the distractions better, they
became too much and took me away from the things I was supposed to be doing.

Early in the season I had the opportunity to talk with Mike
Schmidt of the Philadelphia Phillies. As I mentioned, Mike had
also won two MVP awards in a row; I really respected him as a
player and a person, so I was anxious to hear his advice.
"Mike," I told him, "my spring training was unbelievable." "I
know exactly what you mean," he answered, and then he gave
me some wise counsel. He told me that I owed something to my
employer, to my family, and to myself, and though the people

interviewing me had their jobs to do, I had to keep this fact in mind first and foremost.

"Don't try to accommodate everyone," he said, "because it will drive you crazy. You've got to learn to say no."

As I would find out before the 1984 season was over, learning to say no sometimes is a necessary part of keeping the scales of life in balance. One more lesson I'd learn: There can be life after the MVP.

I wish I had learned these things before the 1984 season started. But because I didn't, I was pretty mixed up on opening day. One part of me was confident and excited to get the season started, while another part felt uncertain and unprepared because of all the off-season and spring training distractions. On one hand, I think I resented all the attention and publicity to the point that I may have been a little afraid of more success, sometimes hoping for a mediocre year so it would all go away. But another part of me felt that pressure to strive for another MVP-type year so much that I started pressing on the field and trying too hard. That part of me said I had to be fantastic in 1984 — or a failure.

I thought at the time that success had brought me all these new problems, and I wasn't sure I enjoyed the success enough to want to cope with the problems that came with it. As I look back I realize it wasn't the success, but the way I handled it that made things rough that year. I wasn't prepared for the extra demands and challenges that come with success. I know now that it's possible to be successful and still keep things in balance and perspective.

As you've probably guessed, this wasn't the best frame of mind to start a season with. I got off to a poor start, one that seemed twice as bad because of the increased expectations. It was that old "fantastic-or-failure" thing. If I got two singles in a game, I found myself getting upset for also making two outs. But most of the time I found myself reading box scores with 0-for-4, 0-for-3, or 1-for-4 numbers beside my name. I was striking out an awful lot, especially in important situations, and that bothered me even more. As the slump stretched into weeks, I started pressing. And, in turn, the slump seemed to get worse. And the more I would press . . . and so on. The team had also started poorly, and I felt I was largely to blame. After a while, I was trying so hard that some of my swings at the plate began to look futile. They weren't even close. And it was beginning to negatively affect the way I ran the bases and played on defense, too.

It was the worst and longest slump I'd had in almost three years. But I'm sure you can understand that the timing of it made this the most painful one I'd ever gone through. Here I thought I now had all the tools I needed to play good, steady baseball for many years to come, and I was hitting around .220 one month into the season. That was almost 100 points less than where I had been in recent years.

A few seasons before, the newspapers would say, "Dale Murphy is in a slump." It was a little simpler—there wasn't as much presure on me to work my way out of it. Now it was, "Two-time MVP Dale Murphy is in a slump." Again, those expectations (and I'm not saying they came only from the media and fans; I placed a pretty heavy burden on myself, as well) seemed to magnify normal frustration into near desperation. "I *have* to break out of this slump *today*," I would say to myself. I'd go out on the field tighter than a watchspring, instead of just relaxing and naturally working my way through it. That aggravated the slump, especially when I came to bat in pressure situations. As the slump continued, I started experimenting with my swing and trying too many different things. I remember going up to the plate and not being able to concentrate at all. I was trying to hit a home run every time up and felt I needed to win the game for our team. The more I let them down, the harder I tried the next time up. But it wasn't working very well. I kept getting down on myself and battling myself. I just wasn't playing with the right attitude.

Joe Torre began to work with me a lot again. He started with my sense of humor. He'd come up to me and in mock seriousness say something like, "Murph, it's absolutely necessary that you win this game for us tonight. Think you could do it?" He knew the pressure I was putting on myself, and allowing others to put on me, and tried to keep me loose. That helped. So did another round of special batting seminars. These sessions proved one thing: My swing was fine in practice. It only fell apart in a game. My problem, like with the throwing situation several years before, was in my mind. I simply had to learn how to deal with the expectations and the pressure. Once more, Joe did everything he could to help me through this rocky stretch. He thought about benching me a few times, but he knew me well enough to realize that I'd worry about that more than if I had a chance to work out of it. For the good of the team, he had to move me from third or fourth down to the sixth spot in the batting order for several games because I wasn't driving in enough runners. But he tried to handle it so even this would be a positive thing: "I just want to take some of this pressure off you," he'd tell me. Again, Joe played a part that came much closer to friend than manager through my trials.

The slump bottomed out in early May, and then things started to get better. In case you were wondering, the questions about a third straight MVP award didn't stop coming through these weeks. Do you know how funny it feels for a fellow hitting .218 to be talking about an MVP?

Thank goodness I finally decided to stop demanding an MVP-caliber performance from myself every day. That award, I knew by now, was out the window for this year. And, thank goodness, my average didn't stay at .218 for the rest of the season. Now I realize that these two things were strongly connected. Once I relaxed, like I did in 1983 and most of 1982, better things started to happen. It wasn't dramatic, but my average started to climb steadily. With it came more home runs and runs batted in. In June my average was back in the .250s and by the All-Star break it was near .280.

It just goes to show you the power of the mind. For much of the time my average was climbing, I was also battling nagging injuries—a jammed ankle, back problems, and a sinus infection. They were bothersome, though not quite bad enough to keep me out of a game. But those physical injuries didn't do nearly as much to hold me back as the psychological injuries I had inflicted on myself at the start of the season. (If I could have just figured out and harnessed the power of my mind from the start of my career, I wonder what I might have done . . .)

I don't want to give the impression that my rebound was a complete recovery. Even with my numbers getting into the decent range by the All-Star break, I was still far from satisfied with my performance. I was striking out too much, and I was leaving too many runners on base in important spots. I know I shouldn't judge myself on where I was at, but where I could have been. There was still a big difference between the two. I knew my game wasn't at the level where it had been in 1983, so I still had some more work to do. I jokingly said to several writers about that time, "There's nowhere to go but up, right?"

Once more I was voted a starter on the All-Star team, but I didn't feel I deserved it this year. I really appreciated the support from the fans, but this time they might have been voting on reputation more than on performance. From my own team, Claudell Washington was having a much better season than I was, and I'm sure there were several others around the league. Ironically, I ended up having my best performance yet, including my first All-Star Game home run.

I wish I could report that things went smoothly for the rest of the season. But not long after the All-Star Game I went into another slump. It wasn't as bad as the one at the start of the season, but it ended in a much more dramatic way. I'll get to that shortly.

My game didn't totally fall apart like it seemed to in April and early May. I was still getting my hits here and there, but not too many when the team needed them. That really bothered me. Over the past few years I thought I had developed into a pretty good clutch hitter. But now I was leaving a lot of runners on base, several times with the game on the line. In fact, I was coming through less than twenty percent of the time with runners on second or third base when just about any hit will score runs.

This wasn't the only source of my frustration. I was still not happy with the balance between my baseball and family lives. I was not keeping the two separated enough and not spending enough time with my family. Nancy had recently lost another baby during pregnancy—the second time in two years this had happened. I couldn't help wondering if all these added pressures on her had contributed to this, although they probably had nothing to do with it.

Even though Mike Schmidt and Nancy had counseled me to learn to say no sometimes, I still found that to be one of the hardest things I'd ever tried to do. I thought that if someone was nice enough to want to talk to me or invite me to their banquet or get my autograph, I didn't want to turn them away. But as time went on, I realized that I could spend almost my entire life accommodating these outside demands, and they'd eventually interfere with my career, as well as my family. I also realized I had allowed that to happen in 1984. I just didn't want to make people feel bad.

You can see that life was a little chaotic both on and off the field for me. When I would fail in a game, I'd often flip my bat and helmet away in disgust. I walked around a lot with my head down, kind of moping, I guess. I just wasn't being myself, and as I mentioned earlier, I wasn't happy at all. It was so notice-able, in fact, that a few of my closest friends called me on the road to give me a little kick in the pants and tell me to keep my chin up. Boy, I thought, what am I doing to myself? I'm not only letting my teammates down, but also disappointing all those people who had come to expect me to act better than this.

Finally, everything hit bottom in that game against the Dodgers, when I took everything out on a poor water cooler. That brought me to my senses. The game had become too big a part of my life. I had allowed it to consume me. Every crucial situation seemed almost a life-and-death matter. It wasn't a game anymore. I had allowed external pressures to affect me, to get to me.

I knew some of those unpleasant changes I'd been thinking about for months would now *have* to come about. With Nancy's help, I made several decisions. They were painful for me, because it meant I'd have to start saying no a little more. Oh, I'd still have time for my baseball obligations, but not quite as much as in the past. It was all part of getting the things back in balance that had been out of whack.

I also made a resolution to relax and enjoy the game more, regardless of how I was playing. I had the security of a good con-tract and enough confidence in my ability to know I could keep a job at this level. I just had to unwind and let it happen.

I had placed too big a burden on myself, and I was now going to unload it. I didn't want to get caught in that "fantastic-or-failure" trap any more. I'd always try my best, and if it brought success, fine. If not, I'd have the comfort of knowing I gave it my all. No longer did I want my mind to get in the way of the quality of my game, except in a positive way.

It had been a humbling several months, and it was a humbl-ing several hours spent thinking and planning to get my priori-ties back on track again. But I can say now that they were some of the best-spent hours of my whole life. Almost immediately, everything turned around for the better. Life was happier at home. I felt more at peace with the Lord. And my game fell back into place, too. Earlier in 1984 I'd had a small rebound from my slump. This time it was a full recovery. I hit almost .350 for the final month and a half. I was fortunate to be named National League Player of the Month for September. Like that same award right after my poor 1981 season, this was especially meaningful.

After so many trying months of hitting in clutch situations, getting a one-hundredth RBI in the final game of the season also meant a lot. When they returned the ball used in that hit to me, I decided to give it to Joe Torre. Joe had done much for me over the previous three years, and I sort of had a feeling this would be his last game as our manager. The Braves had not lived up to expectations in 1984 and finished well out of the pennant race. Sure enough, a few days after the season ended, they let Joe go. I hated to see that happen. Joe had helped me mature so much as a hitter and a player that I owed much of my success to him. He helped me to gain confidence in myself through slumps and helped me to maintain an even keel when I was hitting well. Joe's a great baseball man, and I'm sure there will always be a job for him somewhere.

When I call 1984 my most frustrating season, some people don't understand. They look at my statistics and see what appears to be a good, solid year. But knowing the full story behind it, I think you can see why I feel this way. It gets back to judging yourself on where you can be, rather than where you are. Despite all the frustrations, I managed the second-highest batting average in my career to that point. I hit as many home runs as in both of the seasons when I won the MVP. I had the most extra base hits of any year in my career so far. And here's an odd one: It had been six years since I had hit a home run in the Astrodome, an especially tough place to get them. In 1984 I hit *six* there. Sure, much of this came in those final six or seven good weeks. But, oh, where I could have been . . .

If 1984 was my most frustrating season, it was also in a way my most valuable because of what I learned through it. I just wish I didn't have to keep finding out all these things the hard way!

I learned much about myself and about life, and I tried to make some changes in my attitude that would benefit me the rest of my life.

That should mean 1985 would be among the most peaceful and contented seasons of my career, right?

Well, it was. Though the team didn't play well at all and lost almost 100 games, I still felt good about things. I was pleased with my effort and pleased with the balance I had rediscovered.

We moved to a new home during the off-season before 1985. That was another one of those decisions we made to help me separate my baseball life and family life a little better. Life was more peaceful all around, and I spent a lot more time with my family. Of course, I didn't have an MVP award to deal with this year, but even if I had, I'm confident I would have handled it better this time around.

All of this carried over into spring training, too. It was more like the ones I remember earlier in my career. Sometimes I did wonder what Ryne Sandberg, the 1984 MVP winner, was going through right then. I didn't ever mind the attention, it's just that it got to be a little bit too much for me. But now everything was pretty well back to normal, and I was prepared and raring to go by the time opening day came.

Our new manager was Eddie Haas, a man I was well acquainted with from my years in the minor leagues. Eddie had been with the Braves' organization for years and years. He was a quiet person and didn't say much, but I'd always admired him and was looking forward to playing for him. There was a lot of excitement on the team, for we had added quality players like Bruce Sutter, one of the best relief pitchers in baseball. I was especially looking forward to watching other players try to hit off Bruce rather than face that task myself. Also, it looked like Bob Horner would be back for the start of the season. He had missed all but a month in 1984 with a broken wrist. I feel sorry for Bob. He has tremendous talent, but has been hit with many injuries through his career. A lot of people considered Bob and me kind of a hitting "team," and it would be comforting again to look over from the plate and see him standing in the on-deck circle.

It wasn't long before I got a chance to test the priorities and perspective I had wanted so badly to be a new and permanent part of my life. I had the best start of my career in 1985. Things were going very well for me at the plate again. But with that came the inevitable questions. This time it wasn't whether I could win another MVP award, but if I thought I could become to baseball this year what Wayne Gretzky was to hockey.

Wayne, as many of you know, scores an incredible number of goals and assists, many more than any other player in his sport. And now, after *three weeks* of the season, people were actually figuring out that if I kept this pace up, I'd bat nearly .400, hit 80-some-odd home runs, and knock in more than 230 runs. (To give you an idea of what that means, that would have broken Roger Maris's home run record by about 20 and Hack Wilson's RBI mark by more than 40. In other words, impossible!)

It was a lot like the Braves' long winning streak to open the 1982 season. Because it happened to come at the start of the year, my hitting streak got more attention than it usually would, say, in the middle of August. Some pretty high expectations were developing again. One day, after I got a base hit in a game against Montreal, their first baseman, Dan Driessen, wanted to know if what he had been hearing was true. When I asked him what that was, he said, "That you're going to hit 70 home runs this year."

In past seasons, in fact in just the previous year, articles and talk like that might have affected me and caused me to maybe subconsciously reach for a goal like that. But now I knew better. All I had to do was look at the statistics over my career to see what I was generally capable of. Even if I were to have what I considered to be a great year, I didn't think it would be up there in the category with the best performances in the history of baseball. I was having a nice hot streak, but I knew it wouldn't be possible to maintain a pace like that. I knew I would eventually cool down. I did, but was able to settle into probably my most steady, consistent year yet.

I want to say something about that home-run record. I don't know how Roger Maris managed to hit that many (61) in a season. I think it's one of the greatest individual performances in baseball history. When all this talk started about my possibly making a run at his record, I just laughed. I play in one of the best home-run parks in the major leagues. and I've never hit even 40 in a season. (How many would I have hit so far in my career if I had played in a tough home-run park like the Astrodome?) I don't know if Roger's record will ever be broken. Some of the newer ballparks are tougher to hit home runs in. And with relief pitching developing into such a specialty, and with so many good relievers in the game today, you're almost always assured of batting against a strong, fresh arm. I'm not always concerned when I go into a home-run slump. I may still be swinging the bat well, but just not hitting the ball over the fence. Sometimes home runs are there and sometimes they aren't. And, despite all those early 1985 projections, I knew that through all the streaks and slumps I always seem to end up at about the same place. For me, through most of my career, that's been 35 to 40 home runs and 100 to 120 RBI. That doesn't mean I'd get upset if I hit fewer than that, or be thrilled if I hit more. As long as I'm swinging the bat well and contributing to the team's winning, that's what matters most to me.

I tried to be realistic about things, and that helped me to a smoother season in 1985. Early in the year I was often asked what the difference was that had made me so successful through the first few weeks. Other than my attitude change, I wish I could have answered that question. If I knew what it was, I'd be able to do it all the time. Then I might be able to put some numbers up like Wayne Gretzky!

The change in attitude helped, I'm sure, but that wasn't the whole answer. I do know at the start of the season my team-mates were giving me a lot of opportunities to drive in runs. We were scoring so many runs and they were getting on base so much that I was able to tie the major league record for RBI in the month of April. In fact, I had a chance to break that record on the last day of April, but struck out. All in all, though, I was pleased with my clutch hitting. That was an area I needed to improve on from 1984, and I was happy to get all those oppor-tunities to do it.

The one word I find myself saying most often these days in relation to my baseball goals is *consistency.* I want more than anything to be consistent. I've learned by now that the hot streaks and slumps tend to cancel each other out, and it's what you do in between the two that determines how successful you'll be. That 1985 season is a good example. After the numbers I had in April, you'd expect me to go on to have much better statistics at the end of the year, too. But the season is so long, that things almost always even out in the end. Because of that, baseball is the best sport at providing a true measure of your ability. It's much tougher to have one of those Wayne Gretzky–type seasons when you take the field twice as often as pro hockey and basketball players and ten times as often as pro football players. The law of averages catches up with you more and pulls you down, or up, to the level of your ability.

So, even though I had that real good start in 1985, I ended up hitting only one more home run than in my previous best year and had my *second*-best totals in batting average and RBI.

Yet I can look back with the satisfaction of knowing that, along with 1983, it was my most consistent year in terms of avoiding slumps. It was also consistent with my level of play for the past four years.

Those are the sorts of things I've started looking at more and more. Consistency is something that can only be measured over a long period of time. That "162-game attitude" took me a few years to acquire. But now that I've endured many streaks and slumps, and have matured (I hope) in my approach to them, I *should* be able to produce more consistently. That doesn't mean I don't feel it's important to improve. I do. In baseball though, improvement usually comes in little chunks. I figure through the goals I set and through experience, I'll continue to improve as a baseball player (and as a person, too). But maintaining consistency is something I need to work at day in and day out.

The biggest frustration I had in the 1985 season was the fact that our team had another bad year. Lots of things went wrong, particularly injuries to some of our key players. But we just plain didn't play well, either. It was a poor season for us, and I feel bad that it ended up costing Eddie Haas his job as our manager before the year even ended. Like they say, it's much easier to fire one manager than twenty-five players, but sometimes it's the players who deserve it.

I just mentioned injuries, but for the fourth straight year I was fortunate not to suffer any injury bad enough to keep me out of a game. When I look around and see how many different things can happen to a ballplayer, it makes me feel really blessed. I have an obligation to play in every game I can, and I've been able to appear in more than 650 games in a row going into the 1986 season. Believe me, it's been no doing of mine. I know I've been protected many times from potentially serious injuries and have been allowed to recover from the minor things in time to be able to play in a game. I don't know how much longer this consecutive-games streak will continue, but the Lord has already blessed me in this way far more than I deserve.

Come to think of it, in 1985 he blessed me in *every* way far more than I deserve.

What does the future hold for Dale Murphy?

Of course, being the best possible husband and father is at the top of my list of future goals. Nancy and I both want a large

family, and I know it's going to take a good deal of time to care
for their needs.

I hope I can continue to help building the Church and
serving the Lord. Nancy and I would love to go on a mission
together someday. And I hope this book helps the cause in some
small way. If one person can learn from my experiences and
gain a desire to grow closer to the Lord, it will have been worth
it.

To be honest, I haven't thought as much about my long-
term baseball goals. I usually make them on a season-to-season
basis. I'm not aiming to hit a certain number of career home
runs or bat for a certain average. My most important goal, I
guess, is to be able to look back and know I had a good career,
not just a few good years. That gets back to the consistency I
talked about.

I don't have an exact time frame of how long I'll stay in baseball. Family considerations will always come first. I can see
myself getting to the point, if we have a few more children,
where I'll need to take a close look at the time I might be able to
spend with them if I took a different job. Baseball can be rough
on family life sometimes, but it also allows us to do a lot of
things as a family that other professions don't allow for. If it ever
looked like my baseball career just wouldn't allow me to spend
enough time with the family, I'd call it quits right away.

I'm under contract with the Braves through the 1987
season. The way it looks right now, I'll probably try to sign one
more long-term contract, then think very seriously about
retiring. You never know what will happen. Maybe I'll lift
weights wrong one day and end it all. Maybe I'll lose my game
all of a sudden. Maybe an injury will end my career. You just
never know in athletics. But one more contract could take me
into my mid- to late thirties, about the time most ballplayers are
beginning to slow down. I don't want to drag my career past the
time I'd be useful to the team. I may not be at the peak of my
abilities when I retire, but I don't want to slide too far down the
other side, either.

History says I should be having my best years right about
now. It seems many ballplayers hit a peak in their late twenties
or early thirties, then maintain that level for approximately five
years. I guess that's the time when experience finally matches
up with physical ability. I sure know a lot more about the game
now than when I began in the major leagues in 1977.

When my contract does expire, I hope it works out that I can stay with the Braves. We've grown to love Atlanta and the people here, and you already know how I feel about the organization and what it's done for me. With free agency making it easier for ballplayers to switch teams, not many get to start and finish their careers in the same city. I hope I'm part of that minority.

As I said, I don't have any concrete long-term goals other than developing the consistency that will allow me to look back and be happy with my whole career. I don't feel a great urgency to hit 500 home runs, or to play in a record number of consecutive games. If it happens, great. If not, I believe I could still feel I'd had a good career. Having a .300 career batting average would be nice, for that would show I'd achieved the level of consistency I'm aiming for. Hitting .300 for a season is one of the toughest things for me to do. I've only accomplished that twice in the major leagues — and then only barely. I'm afraid I had a few too many mediocre seasons early in my career to be able to finally reach that .300 lifetime level, but it's something to keep shooting for. When I hit for a good average, everything else seems to fall into place.

Sometimes people wonder if making the Baseball Hall of Fame is a goal of mine. It really isn't. That's something I can't comprehend, and I feel funny even talking about it. To be voted into the Hall of Fame, you have to keep going year after year, and I haven't really proven I can do that yet. If I can be consistent through the end of my career, I might end up with some pretty good numbers, but until I get close to that point I can't seriously think about it.

I guess there is one thing I feel I have to do before the end of my career — play on a winning World Series team. That's every ballplayer's dream. As far as I'm concerned, that's the ultimate goal. Before the 1984 season, when I was being asked all those questions about a third straight MVP, I'd tell people I didn't care if I only hit .200 as long as our team was in the World Series. A month or so into the season, when I was hitting not much above .200, I changed my statement to .250! But the point remained the same. There is no true excitement in baseball until you accomplish something as a team. It's been neat to win those MVP awards, but I'd just as soon be on a world championship team. I've never been on a team that was *the* best.

A few years ago I was invited to present a trophy to the East Marietta, Georgia, team that won the world championship at the Little League World Series in Pennsylvania. Here these fellows were eleven and twelve years old, and they'd already accomplished what I've never been able to in more than twenty years of playing baseball. I sure hope that changes before my career is over.

I've thought about what I'd like to do after my career is over, though probably not as much as I should. I would enjoy being a coach, not on the professional level, but probably at a college or high school. I'd need to get a college degree first, and I'm still four years away from that. But I'd love to be a coach.

Something else inside of me wants to get involved with a really creative endeavor. I enjoyed the few TV commercials I was a part of. I think it'd be fun to be involved in the making of a commercial or a good movie. I think it would be a blast to write a novel.

Who knows? I might end up being a dentist.

As you can see, I haven't nearly made up my mind, but I hope I still have several years to think about it and decide. I'm sure the Lord will direct me to the right places, just as he has all along the way.

Part III

Perspectives

13 Priorities

It was probably the toughest decision I've ever faced.

We were living in our "dream" home in Lawrenceville, a beautiful town about an hour from downtown Atlanta. Everything there seemed to be just right for us. Our neighbors, Chris and Lanell Callaway, were wonderful LDS people we grew extremely close to. The ward was super and the people in our neighborhood very nice. The previous few years had been the best of my baseball career. We felt comfortable with this area as a place to raise our kids.

Just one thing was wrong. We were so visible there in the middle of a subdivision, people frequently came to our house. I was flattered that they wanted to visit us, but I soon realized that I needed to do a better job of separating baseball, which is my job, from my home life. I don't think I'd look at it differently if I were in any other occupation. Just because I am a baseball player doesn't mean I need to bring more work home from the office.

It took some friendly reminders from Nancy for me to realize what I'd known all along—that my family was most important in my life.

I could see I'd have to draw a line. There was my baseball life, and an obligation to the owner and fans who pay my salary. And then there was my family, where the responsibilities were eternal. Time had to be devoted to both. But the two would have to be separated or it would affect the things I cherish most in life.

Needless to say, there were some months of real soul-searching. Finally, we decided that to be able to make this proper separation, we'd need to move to a new home. As I said, it was probably the toughest decision I've ever made. We loved so many things about our house and the area. We wanted the kids to grow up where they could have lots of friends to play with. And we didn't want our associates to think we were withdrawing from the human race or that we didn't want to see them again.

But a priority is a priority, so we moved to a home that has allowed us to enjoy more private family time. It has definitely made a difference. And I think it's helped make me a more relaxed and better baseball player and more able to enjoy the time I spend with the public. (And I do enjoy that time!)

It makes me chuckle when I think of what Rick Reilly said in a *Sports Illustrated* article about this time in our lives — something like "Mr. Clean had to get just a little mean." I hope I'm never mean to anyone, but sometimes I need to take a stand to make sure my life's priorities stay straight.

I wish I could take credit for developing the system of priorities I have. It comes from the gospel and is taught constantly by the Church. Baseball is by no means number one in my life. Our owner, Ted Turner, might not like to hear that, but I think he understands. Don't get me wrong. I love baseball, and I try to give 100 percent of myself to it and to my team. It's important to me that I succeed at it. But I try not to torture myself when I go 0-for-4, and I try not to inflate myself when I go 4-for-4 or hit a home run to win the game. I'm thankful for that perspective the gospel gives me. It helps me when I go home after making a crucial error or not hitting the ball the way I should. It teaches me that Nancy and the kids are my top priority.

The gospel hasn't been my only teacher of family-centered priorities. My father and mother really showed the way in this regard. My sister, Susan, and I always had the feeling we were very important to them. They did so much with us and for us. It would have been easy for them to neglect Susan while we were growing up because my pursuits were so attention-grabbing. But our family also did a lot of camping and outdoorsy sorts of things because Susan enjoyed that. She also loves marine biology, so Mom would spend hours and hours on the beach helping her find specimens.

My parents used to keep scrapbooks with newspaper clippings about my games on the coffee table in the living room. Once while we were in high school, I think, Susan asked in a joking sort of way where her scrapbooks were. That was the last time those books were seen there.

Dad and Mom were always concerned that *both* of us have our own identities and feelings of self-worth. They were always very supportive. And though he probably wouldn't admit it, I'm convinced Dad sacrificed much of his career development by turning down transfers because he wanted me to play baseball for Jack Dunn and no one else. That's really something! I only hope I can be half the father to my kids that he is to me. Mom's support was just as important. She was always at my games, always behind me, always making me feel that I could accomplish anything I wanted to.

It's funny how little things can end up meaning so much to us down the road. Dad used to take me golfing when I was young. I didn't think I enjoyed it too much back then—tromping all over the place, carrying that heavy bag, and wearing big blisters on my hands. But I look back on those times now as being special, and as I grew I could see why Dad was doing it. He wanted us to do something fun *together*. Besides, golf is great for having good, long talks. It became our way of getting off on our own. One night in Cincinnati, early in my major-league career, I called Dad. (I still can't believe I did this!) We had no game the next day, I told him, and I wondered if he wanted to go golfing with me. He hopped in his car and drove through most of the night from Pittsburgh (it's about six hours). We went golfing in Cincinnati—in the rain. I'll always remember that day. I have some big shoes to fill as a parent.

It's very difficult to express myself when talking about my family. They mean so much to me. Nancy is not just my wife, but also my best friend. She is very wise and understanding and patient in putting up with my unusual life-style. It's not easy being the wife of a ballplayer and trying to maintain a stable home atmosphere. But she does it, and takes care of me, too— probably the biggest challenge of all. When I'm on the road, I find I need to talk to her at least once and sometimes three times a day. She has a way of putting everything into perspective when things aren't going too well on the field. I don't know what I'd do without her.

Then there's my other home team — my sons Chad, Travis, Shawn, and Tyson. (We've started our own infield, now that the outfield is full!) I learn so much from these little guys.

Chad taught me a little lesson on priorities one night. We were playing San Diego a few years ago in a game many remember as one of the most fight-filled in baseball history. It seemed that every time we turned around another fight broke out. It was awful — I felt like we were in a hockey game. Well, after each fight the announcer said, "Let's see who gets thrown out of the game this time." Chad was watching all of this on TV, and Nancy would come over after each fight to make sure I wasn't getting into trouble, I guess. After one of the fights, Chad looked over at Nancy and said, "I hope Daddy gets thrown out this time." Nancy was shocked, of course, and she asked him, "Chad, what do you mean by that?" Chad answered, "I hope he gets thrown out so he can come home and play with me."

Believe me, I felt the same way during that game. In fact, I can't think of many things I'd rather do than play with my kids.

Our second boy, Travis, has taught us a different sort of lesson. He was born with Rubinstein-Taybi syndrome. It's a rare condition that slows down the progress kids normally make and causes some health problems as well. Travis has already endured many trials in his young life, and Nancy and I suffer along with him when he does. But there's also great joy when we see him move forward in some small way. They say that people with handicaps are some of our Heavenly Father's most special sons and daughters, and I believe it. Our Travis is certainly one of them; he's very special to us. I'm grateful he came to our home so we could give him the kind of medical care he needs.

We don't talk too much about this, because we realize we're not unusual in having a handicapped child in our home. Many people are called on to work with and help those far more dependent than our son is on us — and under much more difficult circumstances. We admire these people so much and know they will be greatly blessed for their Christlike love and service.

My family *does* come first, but I've learned just how easy it is to forget this simple fact. After the 1983 season I found myself trying to do a few too many things away from home: to help a charity here, which is good; to speak there for a church group, which is good; and to meet these people and do that interview in which the Church will invariably be mentioned, which is good. But all of a sudden I realized I wasn't around Chad, Travis, and Shawn enough. I was doing good things, but I wasn't spending enough time with Nancy.

I now know that there are always good things that can be done, but there are also better things that *need* to be on top, and it all starts at home. Since then I've really tried not to sacrifice these top priorities for the other demands on my time, though they are good and worthy. It's tough to sort through them sometimes, but I find when I go to my Heavenly Father for guidance, he helps me make the right decisions to keep my life in balance.

There's one thing I really dislike about being a baseball player—having to work every Sunday during the season. Sunday is the Lord's day, and no baseball games should be played then. I've had the opportunity to attend Church meetings in cities all across the country. But the spirit I feel while attending a good meeting on Sunday morning is not present when I show up at the ball park. I've learned that there is spiritual strength in *only* attending Church meetings and doing the work of the Lord on the Sabbath.

In my travels, it's strengthened my testimony to see the same gospel in action whether I'm in Philadelphia, Houston, or San Francisco. And I can always count on receiving the same warm welcome I get at my home ward in Atlanta, even though I may not play for their favorite baseball team.

I try to attend as many Sunday meetings as my game schedule allows. I've been blessed to hear enough experiences and lessons to fill a book much larger and more interesting than this. And it sure helps the rest of the day go better. Nothing against Chicago, but I feel a special need to attend church when I'm there. I play center field right below the "Bleacher Bums," a group of fans that can get especially—how shall I put it—boisterous. I need all the spiritual strength I can muster when playing in Chicago!

The Church is the same wherever I go. And so are the people. Whenever I see an elders quorum president ask the brethren to do their home teaching, it reminds me I need to get out and do mine when I get back home. And when I see a

Sunday School teacher go the extra mile to share an inspiring lesson, it makes me more determined to do a better job in my church callings.

Needless to say, serving the Lord and taking an active part in his church is also right at the top of my list of priorities. I feel very fortunate to have found the gospel, and I'm grateful Barry and Stefnie Bonnell took the time to share it with me. Since the Lord has blessed me with so much, I feel obligated to do what I can to serve him.

One calling I feel I always have is to represent the Church the best I can. Since it's well known that I'm LDS, I have to be very careful what I say and do. Unfortunately, my traveling doesn't permit me to hold certain Church jobs, but I'm grateful my bishops have found places where I could serve. In Lawrence-ville, I was in the elders quorum presidency. One of the most important things I learned from that is what I used to tell the brethren quite often: "Please do your home teaching!" I know this is an inspired program, for it provides the only contact some of our members have with the Church.

Not long ago, I was asked to teach an early-morning semi-nary class during the off-season. It's a challenge keeping those inquisitive and enthusiastic young minds interested that early in the morning. Anyone who knows me can tell you I'm defi-nitely not an early morning person, but I was so grateful for this call. One year we studied the New Testament, and I gained a much greater appreciation for the life and mission of the Savior. And I love being around young people. Their enthusiasm helps keep me young, and their questions keep me on my toes.

While on the subject of youth, I'd like to direct a few thoughts especially to them. I know how tough it is to grow up in these times. You're faced with temptations I'd never even heard of when I was in high school (and I'm not that old!). If there's one thing I could say, it would be to stay close to your family and to the Church. These may not be the popular teach-ings of this day, but someday you'll understand. Don't be fooled by those who would knowingly or unknowingly want to change your priorities. Some of these people may even be your friends. Some are definitely not your friends, though, and they'll try to teach you that the gospel is not the best way of life for you. Hang in there! If you aren't sure about it now, I can promise you that someday you will be sure. Kneel and ask your Father in Heaven for help and he'll give you the strength to overcome your temp-tations. He'll also guide you toward such important steps as serving a mission and getting married in the temple. I assure you that you won't ever regret doing the right thing.

I'm frequently asked to speak to Church groups. I'm happy to do it, though giving talks still makes me quite nervous. I'm definitely not a polished speaker. Like Alma, I wish I could express myself with the power of angels, especially in sharing my testimony. Along with my family, it's the most precious thing I have. I know that the Savior lives, that the true gospel has been restored, and that there's a prophet on the earth today. The gospel is true and it's a wonderful way to live our lives. I know that living the gospel will allow us to be safe, productive, and happy. I'm thankful I've had my prayers answered concerning the Book of Mormon and Joseph Smith. I hope everyone reading this will feel how surely I know these things and that I do have a testimony.

Baseball is not most important to me. But it still is an important priority. It's provided me with a great way of life and allowed me to meet people and do and see things I'd never be able to otherwise.

I work hard to succeed at baseball. I owe that to the game, to Ted Turner, to my manager and teammates, and to the fans. I am paid good money for what I do, and I devote a lot of effort toward improving my skills and performance.

Baseball (and other sports, for that matter) is unique because your performance on the job is in the newspaper and on TV and radio for the entire nation to see. And the reaction to something well or poorly done comes on the spot and can be very powerful. There's a great deal of pressure on a baseball player to succeed. The successes and failures are probably magnified more than they should be. But I'd like to think I'd also try to do my best regardless of my occupation.

I don't ever want to leave the impression that it doesn't bother me when I fail in a game. It upsets me a great deal when I make an error or strike out in an important situation. And I get very concerned when I go into a batting slump. I feel I'm letting a lot of people down, and I don't like to do that. I guess what I'm trying to learn is to leave the successes and failures at the ballpark and not take them home with me. It's not easy to do, but I'm sincerely working on it.

Baseball, they say, is a game simple enough to be played by six-year-olds, but complex enough to confuse sixty-year-olds. I learn something new about it every day. Some think you just throw on a uniform and run around the field. But there's much more to it than that. Each moment has so many variables — the pitcher and hitter, the pitch, the catcher, the manager, the weather, the ballpark and playing surface, and so forth. Every game is unique in its situations and challenges.

I consider myself still a student of baseball. It may not be as important as solving the nuclear arms race, but this is the talent and opportunity the Lord has blessed me with and I'm going to do the best I can with it. I know the better I play baseball, the more opportunities I'll have to share the gospel.

That's another reason I decided to get tougher on my priorities a few years ago. I found that too many distractions off the field not only affected my family, but my quality of play on the field. Once I started to concentrate more on the most important things in my life, everything seemed to fall back into place — including my baseball game.

This doesn't mean I feel doing things for others is unimportant. Helping friends and neighbors, pitching in for charities, and serving in the community are among the noblest activities people can engage in. There's another group I feel a special obligation to — the fans. They *do* pay my salary, but it's more than that. There's a unique bond, I feel, between a ballplayer and the people who support him. Signing an autograph, having my picture taken, or making appearances is a small price to pay for the contribution they make to my life. Therefore, it's a priority with me to spend time with the public and to search for ways to help other people.

There's a unique place for each of these things in our lives — family, church, career, others. The challenge for me has been to balance them and keep the most important things on top. Without proper priorities it's easy to lose perspective in life — and that can eventually lead to more serious problems.

That's a lesson I had to learn the hard way.

14 Image

Anyone in as visible a profession as baseball develops an image, consciously or not. Most of the time the image is a lot bigger than the person. Sometimes the two aren't even close.

A public image is an easy thing to gain but hard to shake, so you go about your job and hope the image is a positive one. Much of it is shaped by the media. If you have a rough day at the plate and then blow up in front of reporters in the clubhouse, it's all over the news the next day. It doesn't take long to make a negative impression.

Baseball players seem to project several distinct images: as athletes, as celebrities, and, unfortunately, as extremely wealthy men playing a kids' game.

I think people often have the feeling that since you are making the salary you do that there couldn't possibly be any problems. Sometimes when Nancy tells people how much she misses having me home during the summer, they will say, "You have all that money. What in the world could you have to worry about?" Too often people relate having money to having no cares.

We are grateful for a good income, but things do balance out. Money doesn't just eliminate the challenges in life. In many ways it makes things more complicated. It seems the more you make, the more you have to spend — hiring people to handle the money, taking care of taxes and investments, and so forth.

People begin to see you as a different person once you get to the major leagues and start earning good money. You think you haven't changed, but others around you think you have. In a sense, things do change. You are able to do some things you never dreamed of, but none of it makes you happy or eliminates your challenges.

Being able to afford a vacation to the Virgin Islands — which we would like to visit but have never done so — is a material pleasure. You have it, then it's gone. "Boy, was that neat," you say, and then you're back home and living with your family again, the same as before. The things that make you happy all the time are your relationships with your wife and children and the Lord.

The Church and gospel have made me see those things clearly, and my feelings on family and the Church have contributed a great deal to the public image I have. As a Latter-day Saint I feel that I must not do anything that would reflect badly on the Church. I figure I am going to be an example no matter what I do, either helping someone or affecting them negatively. An athlete is up in front of people, kids are drawn to him, and the impression he makes is important when millions are watching him every night.

Since joining the Church I have realized I have a special message and special blessings, and if I can exemplify that through my actions on the field, I will try to do it.

The challenge is to live a certain way because you believe it is a better way of life, not just so the public will think of you in a certain way. If someone lives his life just to make an image, not really believing in that way of life, he will never be happy.

I think I am being myself when I sign autographs after games or talk with reporters. I don't feel pressure to protect some great image I've tried to create. I really believe the life-style I've chosen is the one that brings true happiness. If it ever got to the point where I was basing my actions on how it would look in the papers — living the way the public expected me to — it would be a frustrating life. There is no way to live up to expectations the media can create. Often I am portrayed as a person who never, ever says no, who is always nice to everyone, who never gets upset at himself or gets down when he has a crummy game.

Sometimes it gets embarrassing. A writer once asked what my faults were, and I said I had too many to list. He said, "Come on, name one." I said, "Well, I do eat too much," so he wrote that one of Murph's only faults is that he eats too much, and wound up by giving the impression, *Don't you wish that was your only fault?*

He meant well, but I felt a little ridiculous because I am just like everyone else. I have problems. I have bad moods. Nancy and I never have any arguments — no, of course not. I never get upset with the kids. I never do that. Sometimes it seems that people really believe that.

They seem to lose touch with reality. I try to be considerate and do the right things, and all of a sudden people think I'm just — I don't know exactly how to put it — just not human. Being on TV tends to make people think you are more than what you are, and that's the embarrassing part.

Sometimes it seems because of baseball everybody has expectations, and due to the publicity, everything gets exaggerated. Do something bad and they say, "Well, Dale Murphy is a crummy guy and a million people saw it." You get a reputation fast when you're on TV. And if you're playing really well — say you're Reggie Jackson hitting home runs in the World Series — the publicity really gets out of hand.

I've tried to show that a player can be a good person and still play baseball. Early in my career it seemed a lot of people thought I wasn't intense enough, because I didn't go bananas out on the playing field. How could I be competitive and still be nice? They didn't realize you can be intense and yet not lose control or get overly aggressive.

Besides, losing control never seems to come to much good. The more upset I get with myself, the more it hurts my play.

During my slow start in 1984 I was only hitting around .200. It started to get to me; I was frustrated. After one strikeout I kicked a plastic watercooler when I went in the dugout, and it made big news in the papers the next day. That made my mistake even worse. Not only had I lost my temper, but then I had to read about it the next day. With the image that is often made of me, anytime I veer from that norm, it gets in the news.

My good friend in Atlanta, Chris Callaway, taught me a fine lesson that same year during the slump. After one out I blindly threw my helmet down.

That night Chris called me at the hotel. "Dale, my kids consider you the Gentle Giant," he started out. "The last couple of games you have shown displays of emotion that weren't the Murph I know. Let those other guys throw their bats and helmets. You exercise patience with dignity. Graciously wait out your slump, because you'll be judged on how you handle the slump far more than when you're doing well.

"I know it's tough to be in a slump. But in the Lord's eyes it likely doesn't matter if you ever get another hit as long as you live. You have your family, your church, your friends. What you stand for is far more important than hitting the ball. I have the luxury of getting mad, because nobody sees it. You don't have that luxury. Millions are watching you when it's a bad day at the office."

I felt ashamed and humbled, and told him he was entirely right.

The next game I hit a home run.

It can be frightening to know how many people are looking up to ballplayers. It is unfortunate that doctors and schoolteachers aren't as heroic in the eyes of kids as athletes. I often think that everybody should have his father as his hero, not a ballplayer he has never met. After all, I am no different than anyone else. That we know from the gospel teachings, and, despite what is involved in an image, the only difference between me and anyone else is that I happen to wear a baseball uniform to work.

15 Media

I guess I would be one of the last players in the major leagues to complain about the type of media coverage he has received. I've been treated well, sometimes to the point where I come off looking like somebody who doesn't make any mistakes, never gets mad, and never does a thing wrong.

Occasionally I'm asked about all the good publicity I've received over the years. I've always felt that if you treat people with respect and as equals they will treat you the same way. I try to be nice to everyone I meet, not to fit an image but because we are taught in the Church that that is the way we should be with people. It makes our lives better and makes those we meet feel better, too.

When dealing with the media, I try not to get myself in a position where I could be ridiculed for something I said. I don't like the idea of building myself up just to be shot down someday. And I don't think bragging about things ever comes to much good. Sooner or later it catches up to you.

Like any other group, ballplayers have a lot of different attitudes. Some seem to thrive on media attention. Reggie Jackson, though I don't know him well, seems to always attract attention, whether he's hitting a home run, glaring at a pitcher, or just talking with the press. Steve Carlton is a nice person from what I know of him, but very private. Both are great ballplayers, but they see things in completely different ways as far as the media is concerned.

So often I see players get upset about what is written—and understandably so. But that is one of the first lessons you should learn in baseball: Media attention is part of the game, and no matter what you did out there yesterday, it will be in the papers today. You learn to accept it.

Once a player learns to work with the media and be truthful and honest with them, they'll be the same with him.

I know some reporters are trying to create a story where there isn't one, but I haven't run across that. Some have asked me questions solely to get a reaction, but I have managed to sidestep those. I just try to learn as I go along, one question at a time.

I try to read the papers fairly regularly, if for no other reason than to see how I am quoted. But normally I don't get too excited over what is said about me because I just try to respect the reporter's job. I'm part of that job—whether I like it or not. If we have mutual respect, it works out well.

Mike Schmidt of Philadelphia also has some good advice when dealing with the media: Don't read the papers when you are going 0-for-4 at the plate.

When you are being scrutinized every day, there are bound to be some conflicts. There are always disagreements on what does and doesn't belong in the public domain.

I've known players who had drug problems and it was printed in the papers. If they are arrested for breaking a law I'm sure it will be made public and that's the price they pay. But if a player privately is trying to deal with, say, a drug or alcohol problem, I think it should remain a private matter. Society seems to have changed so much that every problem a player has—drugs, marriage, whatever—ends up in the papers and on TV.

I've talked to writers who felt the best way for a player to avoid being in the news is not to do that sort of thing, but I don't feel that kind of personal thing should be handled by the news. If the player breaks the law, fine, it's going to be news. But if he is trying to rebuild his life and is taking steps such as going to a rehab center, it should remain private.

The writer may be right in some ways. It may help a player in rectifying or even avoiding a problem if he knows he is responsible to the public for his actions. But in other ways I don't agree that as a public figure your personal problems should also be public.

The relationship between reporters and players can get tough. Every day you see this guy who has to write about your performance, and thousands or millions of people are going to read it. Then you have to come back and talk to the guy the next day.

Sometimes I think a baseball writer has one of the toughest jobs in the world, especially if he is following a losing team. Under those circumstances the writer doesn't get the coopera-tion he gets following a winner. Players get ticked off about what is happening, and it is difficult. When they're winning and everything is fine, everyone wants to talk.

I try to stay at an even keel all the time and to be truthful and cooperative. This goes back to my belief that the Lord has given me a talent to play baseball and sometimes through that I'm able to tell people a little about the gospel. It isn't going to come up in every interview and I'm not going to be preaching, but if I can get some of the philosophy of what I believe in across to the public, that's great. Perhaps somewhere someone will say, "Hey, he's a member of the LDS church," and be interested enough to look into it as I did.

I try to answer questions without forcing my religious views into the discussion, but if the subject of religion naturally falls into a question I am happy to talk about it.

Perhaps my only great difficulty with the media is over the issue of women reporters in the dressing room. That is some-thing I'm not certain will ever be settled.

My first experience with that situation was in 1978 when Barry Bonnell was still with the Braves. We were playing in Atlanta, and after the game a woman reporter walked into the clubhouse.

Barry looked at me and said, "Look, there's a woman coming in. We've got to do something."

I didn't have a lot of answers. "What would you suggest?" I said weakly. After all, what could we do? Call the police? Storm out of the room? Force them out and bolt the door? Shout, "Hey, get those women out of here!"?

Barry went over and told all the reporters they had to leave. He ushered them into a little room off to the side of the club-house. Our public relations people were wondering what was going on.

Barry said he would talk to everyone out there but that he didn't feel it was right to have women inside the dressing room, believing the way he does. He said it wasn't right.

Well, that was the start. Women felt they had a legal right to be there to do their jobs. Some of the players felt they had a right to privacy. Others didn't know what to think, and others didn't seem to care.

The team tried an alternative; they bought us special robes, but that was sort of a joke. It still didn't solve the problem of when to get dressed or when to let women inside.

There were women coming in we had never seen before and never saw again. Maybe just making a point.

It hasn't really happened that much, so I've taken it on a one-at-a-time basis. I've told women I will be happy to talk with them as long as I can — outside the dressing room. I won't talk to them inside.

When women do come in I wait to change until they are gone or dress in my street clothes before they arrive. I can't really make a big deal out of it now because they have won the legal right to be there.

Some women are sympathetic. They come up and say they are embarrassed to be expected to go in there and interview people. Others say being barred from the room would put them at a disadvantage, that they have a right to write about baseball on the same terms as male reporters. But I wonder why they can't see the players have rights too.

I've even had women go so far as to ask why I don't worry about men being in there, but reject the idea of women being allowed inside. They think it's weird and just don't see a difference.

So it has become a tough legal case from my standpoint. It seems to be their legal rights versus my moral rights. A hard situation, but a stupid one to have to be made for us.

I continue talking with women in interview rooms or outside because I believe their rights end where they invade my personal right to privacy.

Even so, the publicity I've received has been good, but I try to take it either way as it comes. You win some, you lose some, but the writer has a job and — like it or not — I'm part of it every day.

16 Life-style

The minute I put my signature on a professional contract, my life changed.

Boy, did it ever!

I had been taught proper baseball skills by some of the best coaches around. But no schooling could prepare me to deal with the life-style of baseball. Getting used to it was sort of like becoming a parent. No matter how many people you talk to or how many books you read, most of your knowledge comes from the schools of experience and hard knocks. Becoming a parent and a professional baseball player share something else in common: Both require some pretty major changes and adjustments to your life.

Many people think baseball players lead a mysterious, exotic life-style. It may be unique, and even unusual, but certainly not exotic. Baseball does have its unusual demands and challenges, especially if you have a family, but they're nothing that can't be overcome with some planning and a little extra effort. Then again, there isn't an occupation that *doesn't* have its own challenges.

Still, from the sort of questions I'm often asked, I realize a lot
of people are pretty curious about the kind of life a major league
ballplayer like Dale Murphy leads.

In many more ways than not it's like yours. I enjoy working
around the house and in my garden. I sometimes step on toys
and peanut butter sandwiches my kids have left on the floor. It's
a mad dash on Sundays to get the whole family ready on time
for church. I enjoy watching a good ballgame on TV.

But I don't think these are the kind of things you want to
read about. You're probably more interested in how a baseball
player spends his days, the association ballplayers have with
each other, what being in the public eye is like, and what effect a
baseball career has had on my family.

Okay then, here goes:

Anyone who travels a lot can tell you that life on the road is
not glamorous at all. We play eighty-one games away from
Atlanta during each regular season, and by the time off days
and travel time are thrown in, it adds up to about three months
away from home, or about half the time between April and early
October. The trips are anywhere from three to fourteen days
long.

How is life on the road? I hate to disappoint anyone, but it's
usually pretty slow and lonely, with not too much going on.
There's nothing wrong with the hotels, or the cities, that we
stay in. Travel conditions couldn't be better. But after several
years of traveling to the same eleven places, I've run out of most
of the sightseeing there is to do. Besides, I'm really there to play
a game, and it would be unfair to my team if I wore myself out
by running around too much. Most of the hotels we stay in are
near the stadium, which is usually downtown, and our sightseeing is pretty well confined to those places we can easily walk
to.

One description I've heard about a baseball player's eating
habits is that he has breakfast at noon, lunch at 3:00 P.M., and
dinner at midnight. That's a little exaggerated, but not much.
We do keep some pretty odd hours.

On the road I usually get up about 10:00 A.M., but that
depends on how long or demanding the previous night's game
was. For instance, we played one game during the 1985 season
that, because of rain delays and extra innings, didn't end until
after 3:00 A.M.! I did a little extra sleeping the next morning.

I grab some breakfast, then, depending on the city, often
take a short walk to loosen up and clear out some of the cob-

webs. If something strikes my fancy while I'm out, I'll stop to take a look.

But even then I'm left with several free hours after I get back to my room. I try to eat lunch about three o'clock and take a half-hour nap after that. Then, of course, there's the daily telephone call home to talk to Nancy and the kids. Much of the rest of the time is spent reading—scriptures, Church books, the newspaper, books about a new topic I'm interested in. I'm also a big fan of old movies, and if a good one is on I'll sit down and watch it (especially if my favorite actor, Jimmy Stewart, is in it).

The team meets at about five o'clock and takes a bus to the ballpark. Batting practice starts at six. Night games usually begin at seven-thirty, so we have two and one-half hours to get dressed and warmed up—about the same length of time an average game will last. Gametime brings a sudden shift in gears —from the slow pace of the rest of the day to an intense, hectic one. Baseball is unusual among professional team sports in that it's the only one not tied to a clock. You just keep playing until nine innings are finished. A pitchers' duel can end in less than two hours, while a big hitters' game or one that goes into extra innings can stretch past three, four, or even five hours. Rain is another factor unique to baseball. It can shorten or lengthen a game, depending on how long and how hard it comes. Somehow we almost always manage to squeeze 162 games in each year, though when and how we do it can be pretty unpredictable.

But things become predictable again after the game. We shower and get dressed. The media come in the clubhouse for interviews. They're in a hurry because of their deadlines, so these conversations usually last only five to ten minutes. And if you didn't particularly distinguish yourself in the game (for good or bad), reporters will probably pass right by you. The team bus leaves forty-five minutes after the game.

Even though a light buffet is served in the clubhouse right after the game, many players (myself included) find they've worked up a bigger appetite, so they'll usually go out for a late dinner. This is a good winding down time, too. Sometimes sleep doesn't come easily after playing an exciting game in front of many thousands of energetic fans. But sleep does come sooner or later, most of the time well after midnight.

Life on the road doesn't always fit into this routine. Day games come along and your schedule flip-flops, leaving you free hours at night. Doubleheaders mean more time at the ballpark.

Rainouts and off days may mean no time there at all. And after two to four days, it's time to move on to another hotel in another city — or head home.

I'm always happy when the destination is home. Sure, I usually need to wake up earlier to help Nancy get the kids off to school. And it's tougher to grab naps sometimes. And there are always errands to run and things to do around the house. But for the privilege of being around Nancy and the kids, these are small prices to pay. The team arrives at the ballpark and takes batting practice an hour earlier than when we are on the road. But again, it's a small price to pay to be able to sleep in your own bed, eat a post-game dinner in your own kitchen, and walk around the familiar surroundings of your own home.

The baseball year begins in late February, when we pack up and leave for spring training in West Palm Beach (near Miami), Florida. I say *we,* because Nancy and the kids come along with me. That alone makes spring training enjoyable. And it is fun. Even though we play about thirty exhibition games, most are either at our training complex or at another team's nearby. I don't spend a lot of time away from the family.

We return to Atlanta in early April, a few days before the regular season begins. Six months and 162 games later, it ends. There isn't a baseball player, though, who wouldn't mind stretching his season another three weeks into late October — to play in the league playoffs and World Series.

Then comes the bonus: an off-season that lasts until it's time to leave for spring training again. In other words, a summer vacation in winter.

Baseball players aren't much different from co-workers in most any other company. Some become good friends, but most remain as acquaintances.

There seems to be a popular notion that since we are on a baseball *team,* we do everything together as a team. That's not the way it is. These days, most of us have our own hotel rooms when we're on the road. And with the exception of a movie or a meal here and there, I'm usually on my own away from the ballpark. Many other players operate the same way.

It's not that we don't like each other. All you'd have to do is come to the clubhouse and hear five minutes worth of the lively banter to see that we get along just fine. But there's a need for privacy away from work, just as in any other job.

Ah yes, the clubhouse. If anything sets us apart from the typical workplace, this does. It can be a mighty lively room, especially when the team is winning. Often there's a lot of kidding and joking (even the practical variety) going on. Maybe it's a form of gallows humor, because there's a lot of pressure on us once we step on the field. But it keeps us loose and laughing, and that's a real service.

I do my share of kidding with the other players, and take my share in return. One day (this was a few years after my throwing problems as a catcher) a reporter asked me which positions I had played. I told him I'd been a first baseman, I'd been an outfielder, and I'd been a catcher. Just then Bruce Benedict, a catcher himself, leaned over and said, "*That's* a matter of opinion." Bruce has managed to kid me about everything from my hearty eating habits to my size-thirteen feet. He's from Nebraska, which makes him an automatic Cornhusker football fan. Of course, being LDS I've adopted BYU as one of my favorites. He often jokes about the "little church schools." He'll ask, "Who are you playing this week, William and Mary?" I usually respond that we could win all of our games, too, if we didn't have to pay attention to little details—like going to school.

One of baseball's most legendary jokesters is Dodger manager Tommy Lasorda. It seems everyone has a Lasorda story to tell, so I'll add mine to the collection:

Tommy is a master of loosening people up and keeping them off guard at the same time. We were on the bus riding to my first All-Star Game, and I was pretty nervous about the whole thing. Tommy turned to Chuck Tanner, who was then managing in Pittsburgh, and said something like, "Chuck, do you remember that time two years ago when you told me Murphy would never make it, and I kept telling you that you were wrong?" Of course Chuck had never said any such thing, but we both got a pretty good laugh out of it.

Here's another one: A few years ago I was signing an autograph for a young boy. Tommy walked past and asked him, "You think that autograph is worth something?"

The boy said, "Yeah."

Tommy responded, "Ten years from now it will be worth a lot less."

Players don't always get along this well. Baseball is a high-pressure job, and a lot of different personalities make up a team.

Nerves and tempers get frayed sometimes over the course of a long, hot summer. But humor helps to keep things going smoother, and the clubhouse is the center of it all.

For the most part, relationships with players on other teams are limited. You only get a few moments to chat here and there — around the batting cage maybe, or on base after getting a hit. That's why the All-Star Game is such a treat. It gives you a better chance to get to know players you've admired for years or young players just making their impact on the game.

I feel a natural closeness to the other LDS baseball players, but I don't get that many chances to socialize with them. When I'm on the road, that means they're at home and are enjoying some well-earned time with their families. But I do follow their careers closely, and really enjoy what chances we get to talk.

It's not easy to develop close friendships in baseball. Players come and go so much. There's not much time for socializing during the season, and between seasons everyone goes their separate ways, many to off-season homes in other states (or countries) or on long family visits and vacations.

There still is a great comraderie among us. I've met and played with many fine men whom I count as friends, and whom I'm sure I'll keep in touch with long after our careers are over.

There's another distinctive aspect to the baseball life-style, and for that matter the life-style of any occupation that has a high public profile: The player's relationship to that public.

Thank goodness for baseball fans. Because of them I'm able to do what I love as a profession. We give them entertainment and hopefully a couple of hours when they can forget about their, and the world's, troubles. And they give us much in return. Fans help pay my salary, and I never forget that fact. But they do a lot more.

Playing in Atlanta is a little different than most other places because nearly all of our games are sent by cable TV all over the United States and parts of other countries. Many people who don't have major league teams close to them have adopted the Braves as their favorite. I've been the recipient of many kind gifts from people all over the country. My reputation as a big eater must be widely known, because I'm often handed cookies, cakes, eclairs, and pies before games — both in Atlanta and on the road. I'm sure many of these come from local LDS people.

I've also had T-shirts, paintings, afghans, pictures, and

other mementos mailed to me. One fan from Alaska even sent me some salmon. A lot of time, expense, and love have obviously gone into many of these gifts. I'm grateful to receive them, but sometimes I wish people would have spent that time and effort on someone who really needed it. They already do enough for me through their support of our team.

If I had five hundred pages I couldn't tell you about all the great people I've met through baseball. How can you describe the feeling when an elderly widow thanks you for bringing companionship to her through your games? or the emotions you experience inside when you meet a crippled youngster who is battling for his life and whose final wish was to meet you?

Being a public figure can make you lose perspective if you don't watch it. People do recognize and make a fuss over you sometimes. Dozens of fans wait to catch a glimpse of you or get your autograph after games. You're invited to make a lot of appearances and speeches. You receive fan letters in the mail every day. It's easy to lose sight of who you really are if you allow yourself to take all the attention to heart.

I remember what a big thrill I got as a young player when someone would recognize me or want my autograph. Fame brings a big change to your life. It came rather suddenly for me, in the midst of the '82 and '83 seasons when I won the Most Valuable Player awards. I still enjoy being in the public eye, but I've found I need to always work hard to keep it all in perspective. I'm no different from the people who seek my autograph. It's just that I wear a baseball uniform and have had some success at the game. Our society happens to make this type of person famous. But it doesn't mean I'm any more worthy of praise or respect than anyone else who works hard at doing something well.

Being well known has its problems. The public can take so much of your time that it can affect other things you should also be doing. When I was first with the Braves I would sometimes spend an hour after games signing autographs and having my picture taken with fans. I still try to be as accommodating as I can at the ballpark, but over the years I've had to cut down the amount of time I spend doing this. I was sometimes late for batting practice, late for team meetings, late getting home. It has taken a long time to learn how to tell people when it's time for me to get to the clubhouse or to go home. I've tried to keep commitments away from home to a happy medium, too. In fact, the Word of Wisdom's reminder of "moderation in all things" has served as a good guide for the time I spend with the public.

Sometimes privacy can be tough to come by, though that isn't as big a problem now as it used to be. I strongly believe in separating my career and family lives as much as possible. But a few years ago that was getting pretty hard to do. Usually these visits to our home were just efforts by well-meaning people to let me know they appreciate me. As a result, we made some adjustments, including moving to a new home, and they have helped.

My career also affects my family in subtle ways. One time when I was signing autographs at spring training, Chad told Nancy he was worried I'd go home with the crowd. I want everyone in my family to feel important. Sometimes that's difficult when Dad is always the one on TV or in the newspaper, or Dad is the one people recognize in public. It's something I always need to be mindful of.

There will be other challenges, too. Though at first my children may be known as "Dale Murphy's kids" at school, I hope they'll be given a chance to develop their own individuality and channel their own paths. And when they come to see my games at the ballpark, I hope they won't be harmed by the not-so-nice things some fans may yell at me, or other derogatory things they may see on TV or read in the newspaper. It all comes with the territory, I realize, but I don't want my family to suffer because of my career. I know with some extra effort and diligence on my part, they won't.

It has its challenges, but I enjoy my life with the public. For a player, there's nothing to compare with the kind of appreciation fans can offer you. After all the money and publicity are gone from an athlete's life, the best memories are usually connected with the fans.

Well, that's a look at the life Dale Murphy leads. I've been blessed with so much through the years: great, supportive parents and sister; loyal friends; the true gospel of Jesus Christ; the strength to overcome adversity; a career I truly enjoy; and a family I cherish and love more than all else.

To sum it all up I can think only of the title of my all-time favorite movie:

It's a Wonderful Life.